The Institution Builder's Toolbox

The Institution Builder's Toolbox

Strategies for Negotiating Change

Jeswald W. Salacuse

BUSINESS EXPERT PRESS
Leader in applied, concise business books

First published in 2024 by
Business Expert Press, LLC
222 East 46th Street, New York, NY 10017
www.businessexpertpress.com

ISBN-13: 978-1-63742-594-7 (paperback)
ISBN-13: 978-1-63742-595-4 (e-book)

Business Expert Press Corporate Governance Collection

First edition: 2024

10 9 8 7 6 5 4 3 2 1

To Donna,
my companion on our journey in five continents and six decades

Description

Both at work and in our private lives, we are often called upon to build new institutions or to renovate old ones, from creating a subsidiary for a corporate employer to forming an investment fund for clients, from working with neighbors to establish a charter school to helping friends organize an athletic club. Drawing on his remarkable six-decade career of building institutions around the world, Jeswald W. Salacuse, a distinguished educational leader, experienced corporate director, noted international arbitrator, and consultant to governments, foundations, and companies, has written a book to guide people skillfully through the challenges of institution building, from shaping and articulating the institutional vision to securing the resources to make it happen. *The Institution Builder's Toolbox: Strategies for Negotiating Change* succinctly breaks down the building process into seven tasks or phases and gives institution builders the tools to successfully accomplish their goals. In an original insight, Salacuse recognizes the crucial and pervasive role that negotiation plays in the institution-building process and advises readers on how to negotiate each of the seven developmental phases to build robust institutions.

Keywords

leadership; bilateral negotiation; multilateral negotiation; privatization; governance

Contents

Also by Jeswald W. Salacuse xi

Preface xiii

Chapter 1   The Nature and Significance of Institutions 1

Chapter 2   Institution Builders 13

Chapter 3   The Elements of Negotiating Institutions 21

Chapter 4   The Seven Tasks of Institution Building 33

Chapter 5   Task #1: Launching the Institution-Building Process 39

Chapter 6   Task #2: Negotiating an Institutional Vision 47

Chapter 7   Task #3: Negotiating an Institutional Plan 55

Chapter 8   Task #4: Negotiating Institutional Resources 71

Chapter 9   Task #5: Legalizing the Institution 83

Chapter 10   Task #6: Promoting the Institution 93

Chapter 11   Task #7: Negotiating Knowledge 101

Chapter 12   Finishing Touches 109

Notes 113

References 115

About the Author 117

Index 119

Also by Jeswald W. Salacuse

Real Leaders Negotiate! How to Gain, Use, and Keep the Power to Lead Through Negotiation

Negotiating Life: Secrets for Everyday Diplomacy and Deal Making

The Three Laws of International Investment: National, Contractual, and International Frameworks for Foreign Capital

The Law of Investment Treaties (3 editions)

Seven Secrets for Negotiating with Government

Leading Leaders: How to Manage Smart, Talented, Rich, and Powerful People

The Global Negotiator: Making, Managing, and Mending Deals around the World in the Twenty-First Century

The Wise Advisor: What Every Professional Should Know About Consulting and Counseling

Making Global Deals: Negotiating in the International Market Place

The Art of Advice: How to Give it and How to Take it

International Business Planning: Law and Taxation (With W.P. Streng, six volumes)

Social Legislation in the Contemporary Middle East (Co-editor with L. Michalak)

An Introduction to Law in French-Speaking Africa: North Africa

An Introduction to Law in French-Speaking Africa: Africa South of the Sahara

Nigerian Family Law (with A. B. Kasunmu)

Preface

"What you are doing here is institution building. You're an institution builder," concluded Harvard Law School Dean Irwin Griswold at the end of a dinner conversation in Zaria, Nigeria, where I was working as a Peace Corps Volunteer to help establish the Northern Region's first law school. Griswold was on a fact-finding mission to examine African legal education. I nodded hesitantly, since, up to that point, I had never thought of myself as "an institution builder," had never been called that by anyone, and was not altogether sure what "institution building" entailed.

That conversation took place in the fall of 1963, just a few months after my graduation from Harvard Law School. During the next six decades, my career would lead me to engage in a wide range of institution-building activities both in the United States and abroad. Some succeeded. Some failed. Today, looking back on that experience, I can now quite comfortably say that I am an institution builder.

During my two years in northern Nigeria, in addition to helping establish a university law school, I worked to develop a diploma program for what were called "native court judges," officials with limited formal education who administered justice throughout that vast territory. Later, I would spend three years in the Democratic Republic of Congo to create a research center on public administration; then three years in Beirut, Lebanon, as the Ford Foundations' advisor on law and development; and after that, three more years in Sudan to establish the Ford Foundation's office and development program for the country. In the years thereafter, I had numerous other foreign assignments, including assisting Egypt's efforts to attract foreign investment, helping Laos write of a new corporation law that eventually led to the creation of its stock exchange, advising the University of Jordan on the establishment of graduate legal education, helping Saudi Arabia train government lawyers, evaluating legal reforms in eastern Europe after the fall of communist governments, and working on a strategy for reforming Indonesia's legal system.

In the United States, I served as dean of the Southern Methodist University Law School and of the Fletcher School of Law and Diplomacy at Tufts University, positions which, by their nature, demand institution-building efforts of their occupants. In addition, I participated in the creation of the India Fund, a closed-end mutual fund listed on the New York Stock Exchange that invests in Indian companies and of various other mutual funds investing in developing countries; served as the founding president of the Association of Professional Schools of International Affairs (APSIA); led the creation of the faculty senate at Tufts University and served as its first president; and worked with the National Center for State Courts to create a leadership academy for state court judges. For over 20 years, I held positions as an arbitrator and president in several international arbitration tribunals, institutions designed to settle disputes between governments and foreign investors. Each of my many assignments was an exercise in institution building. In some cases, I worked to create new institutions and in others, to improve or expand existing entities.

While my experiences in institution building have ranged over five continents and a broad diversity of activities, they had important similarities, similarities that allowed me over time to develop a set of principles for carrying out institution building in many differing circumstances. The aim of this book is to share those principles and their applications with readers to give them the skills to pursue their own efforts at institution building, whether they are parents working to create a charter school, athletes hoping to establish a sports club, investors desiring to launch an investment fund, or corporate executives seeking to form a semiautonomous subsidiary for their company. Efforts to bring about desired change invariably require an institution to carry out that task. For that reason, the subtitle of this book is "Strategies for Negotiating Change." Failure to attend to the institutional requirements of change almost always frustrates the attainment of worthy goals.

Three factors distinguish this book from other works on institution building. First, this book seeks to teach people to build institutions that will help them, an element usually omitted from studies on the role of institutions in economic development and social change. Second, it breaks down the building process into seven phases or tasks that institution builders must successfully accomplish to create a desired institution and identifies the tools that they will need to accomplish their goals. Third, the book recognizes the crucial role that negotiation plays in institution building and advises readers on how to negotiate each of its seven developmental stages to create robust institutions.

I am grateful to Professors Daniel Shapiro of Harvard University and Alnoor Ebrahim of Tufts University for their many valuable comments on the manuscript of this book.

Jeswald W. Salacuse
Cambridge, Massachusetts
March 1, 2024

CHAPTER 1

The Nature and Significance of Institutions

In none of my efforts at institution building did I lay a brick, dig a foundation, or erect a wall. In fact, none of my work had much to do with the physical structures that most people associate with the word "institutions," structures like imposing courthouses, shimmering laboratories, and towering office buildings. Those things are just physical manifestations of institutions. They are not the institutions themselves or their essence that institution builders must create to succeed at their task.

Definitions

Numerous scholars have sought to capture that essence in definitions. Douglass C. North, recipient of the Nobel Prize in economics for his work on institutions, defined them as "the rules of the game in a society, or more formally, are the humanly devised constraints that structure political, economic and social interaction."[1] A somewhat similar definition is that "… institutions are also defined as structures of societal features that direct, empower, or restrain the activities of persons."[2] In short, an institution is a mechanism that society has devised to influence the behavior of its members in desired ways. Some institutions, such as written constitutions, are created by formal decisions of a social group, such as a constituent assembly, whereas others, such as merchant rules for conducting international trade, are based on accepted practices within the merchant community that evolve over time.

Although important, scholars' definitions often fail to capture at least two important dimensions of institutions—their organizational and dynamic qualities. The aim of all institutions is to influence human behavior in desired ways. To accomplish that task, they need an organizational structure endowed with the power to act, which usually requires that institutions employ other humans with the skills and physical resources necessary to influence the behavior of other people. Institutions usually constrain or encourage certain types of human behavior through norms and rules. To be effective, institutions must include individuals or groups with authority and means to enforce those norms and rules. For example, one of the purposes of courts is to enable disputants to resolve their conflicts without resorting to violence. The aim of schools is to encourage members of society to devote the time and effort necessary for them to gain the knowledge to be productive members of that society, enabling their society to prosper. The objective of the institution of land ownership is to encourage farmers to till their land peacefully and to invest their effort and capital to create a productive enterprise because they believe that the law will prevent another person from seizing their holdings. Anytime countries embark on political, economic, or social change, their governments almost always seek to build new institutions or modify old ones.

Sociologists have traditionally divided social institutions into five major types: (1) the family, which is considered the primary social institution; (2) government and the state; (3) the economy; (4) education; and (5) religion. Each of these institutional types may be broken down into subcategories. For example, economists have subdivided the institution of the economy into five subcategories: (1) private property; (2) free markets; (3) competition; (4) division of labor; and (5) social cooperation.

A particular characteristic of all institutions is their intended durability. Derived from the Latin word *instituere*, meaning to establish or to set up, institutions are not intended as temporary arrangements but are meant to last a long time and are therefore designed to have staying power. Constantly preoccupied by the questions of institutional stability, institution builders throughout history have devised various mechanisms that they hope will assure longevity for their creations. Inevitably, changing circumstances lead to the modification or complete elimination of what once had seemed permanent institutions in certain societies, like slavery in America, serfdom in Russia, and apartheid in South Africa, all of which required violent action by members of those societies to end those institutions and replace them with new institutions that hopefully would foster human freedom.

While not all institutions are forged in war and revolution, most are born in some kind of social conflict because the creation of new institutions is invariably perceived as having a negative effect on the interests of some group within the affected society. Thus, a community's public-school teachers may view the creation of a local charter school as harming their interests by taking students and resources away from public schools, and the adoption by that same community of road traffic lanes dedicated to bicyclists is likely to be opposed by motorists fearful that the change will lengthen their time commuting to and from work. The public-school teachers and commuting motorists may organize to oppose these new institutions and, if powerful enough, stop both innovations dead in their tracks.

The implications of these two examples for institution builders are that despite the great potential benefits to the community of the institution you are trying to build, you should not become so enchanted by your invention that you neglect to see opponents waiting in the weeds to ambush you. To avoid ambushes, institution builders should constantly ask: Whose interests will my new institution harm and in what specific way? They should also remember the wisdom of Nicolo Machiavelli (1469–1527) expressed in *The Prince*:

> there is nothing more difficult to plan, more uncertain of success, or more dangerous to manage than the establishment of a new order…for he who introduces it makes enemies of all those who derived benefits from the old order and finds but lukewarm defenders among those who stand to gain from the new one[3]

Regardless of definitions, economists generally believe that a country's pace of economic development is directly influenced by the quality of its institutions. Good institutions protect property rights, foster investment and trade, and control governmental corruption, all of which are necessary for strong economies. Strong institutions are also essential for good governance. The World Bank's widely applied Worldwide Governance Index focuses on six factors of a country's governmental system: (1) voice (i.e., voting) and accountability, (2) political stability and absence of violence, (3) governmental effectiveness, (4) regulatory burden, (5) rule of law, and (6) freedom from corruption.[4] Each of these governance qualities requires strong, effective institutions.

The work of institution builders often focuses on creating new "rules of the game" to be enacted in countries' legal systems, rules whose fundamental purposes are also to influence human behavior. The legal system in many countries is not limited to the formal written laws enacted by legislatures and decisions made by courts but also includes the unwritten customs and traditions of their people. Customs and traditions governing family matters, land tenure, and political organizations in rural areas were also intended to regulate human interactions and were therefore important parts of the institutional frameworks in Nigeria, Congo, Indonesia, and other developing countries in which I worked.

Because institutions have the power to influence human behavior, governments often use them not just to preserve domestic peace and security but also to secure desired behavioral changes in their populations, changes that will hopefully lead to increased prosperity and well-being for their people. They, therefore, devote significant resources to building institutions to attain these goals. For example, the U.S. government has created a variety of institutions to achieve various social ends, such as the Securities and Exchange Commission (SEC) to protect investors and strengthen financial markets, the Environmental Protection Agency (EPA) to guard the country's natural environment, and the Equal Employment Opportunity Commission (EEOC) to protect workers against illegal discrimination. Outside the United States, with the end of colonialism in Africa and Asia and the disappearance of communism in Russia and eastern Europe, new governments in varying degrees declared "development" as a national goal and actively engaged in a process of building institutions that would enable them to attain this goal. Studies by the World Bank and the United Nations have demonstrated that strong institutions have contributed to poverty reduction in many countries. On the other hand, other studies have identified a connection between weak institutions and civil and political violence. Throughout history, human beings have created institutions to establish order and reduce uncertainty.[5]

As Machiavelli foretold nearly 600 years ago, new institutions are not uniformly welcomed in the societies for which they are intended. Various groups within a society often fear that a new institution may negatively affect their interests. For example, beginning in the 1980s, while many governments enthusiastically built new institutions to privatize state enterprises providing public services like electricity, transportation, and water in the hopes that new foreign capital and technology would modernize those enterprises, labor unions and social welfare organizations often opposed privatization, fearing it would result in the loss of jobs and an increase in the price of needed goods and services. In planning for the introduction of new institutions, institution builders should, therefore, identify potential sources of political opposition and seek strategies and tactics to cope with them.

Institutions fall into one of two categories: "governmental institutions," created by a government's action and usually part of its administrative apparatus, and "civic institutions," created and governed by groups of individuals not directly controlled by a government. The former includes courts, regulatory agencies, and state corporations. The latter consists of labor unions, churches, private schools, private corporations, and many other organizations in a country's "private sector," variously defined. The former is usually introduced into society from the top down; the latter emerges from the bottom up.

The Institution-Building Process

While many scholars have studied the impact that institutions may have on society, relatively few have examined how institutions come into existence and specifically how they are built. Implicit in this omission seems to be an unstated assumption that the process of institution building is much the same from case to case and that the process of institution building is less important than the institution itself or its impact on the society for which it is intended. Institution building is a *process,* which one may define as "a systematic movement toward a defined end." How the process of institution building is carried out can directly affect the nature of the intended institution and its ultimate impact on the society for which it is intended. This book, therefore, focuses mainly on the often-overlooked issue of the techniques of institution building. In particular, it explores the *tools* of institution building. Any builder, whether of gigantic skyscrapers or delicate watches, needs tools to do the job. One may define a tool as an instrument or device used to carry out a particular function. In the realm of institution building, useful tools fall into two categories: *physical* tools, like hammers and cranes, which are designed particularly to change the physical environment, and *social* tools, such as meetings and communications, which are designed to affect social relationships between individuals and groups. This book will examine particularly the social tools of institution building that should have a place in every institution builder's toolbox, whether they are educators seeking to build universities, athletic coaches trying to create winning teams, or entrepreneurs hoping to launch money-making ventures.

Individuals who embark on the process of institution building need to be aware that three fundamental principles should guide their work. The first principle of that process, which all institution builders must recognize, is that institution building requires *collective action*. No institution builder, no matter how talented and powerful, can build an institution by acting alone. The initial task for any institution builder is therefore to identify the people who can help and then convince them to join the institution-building effort. At the same time, the introduction of many individuals, each with their own interests, wills, and perspectives, into the institution-building process creates a "collective action problem," which can only be resolved by effective leadership. Institutions do not spontaneously spring into existence. They need individuals with the proper skills and vision to lead the process.

The second principle and a corollary of the first is that institution builders must *negotiate* to achieve their goals. Indeed, they do so to such an extent that one may say that institution building is essentially a process of negotiation and that institution builders must be effective negotiators if they are to succeed in building anything. Negotiation, as I have previously written,[6] can be defined as "a process of communication by which two or more people seek to advance their individual interests by agreeing on a desired course of action." Negotiation is therefore an institution builder's vital tool. Unlike many commercial deals which are often bilateral in nature, institution building is usually a *multilateral negotiation*, an exercise involving many parties, requiring special skills beyond those used in ordinary two-party dealmaking, one of the most important of which is the skill of forging coalitions.

The third principle of institution building is that, to the maximum extent possible, the people who will be served by a new institution should particpate in its creation. Such participation gives the new institution legitimacy and heightens the likelihood that the new institution will meet the needs of the people it will serve and that they will use it willingly rather than seek to avoid it. Similarly, although international development agencies have often urged developing countries to adopt western institutions, experience has shown that countries that adopt foreign institutions without adapting them to the context in which they have been transplanted are often doomed to failure. Institution building is context specific.

The following case illustrates the importance of adhering to these principles in creating an institution of faculty governance for a major university.

Building a Faculty Governance Institution for Tufts University

Established in 1852, Tufts University in Medford, Massachusetts, today has over 13,000 students and 800 faculty members located on three geographically separate campuses that house its eight principal schools: (1) the Medford Campus, located in a suburb of Boston, which houses the School of Arts and Science, the School of Engineering, and the Fletcher School of Law and Diplomacy; (2) the Boston Campus, located in the center of that city, which contains the School of Medicine, the School of Dental Medicine, the Friedman School of Nutrition and Science Policy, and the Tufts Graduate School of Biomedical Sciences; and (3) the Grafton Campus, 45 miles west of Boston, the site of the Cummings School of Veterinary Medicine. While each of Tufts schools has its own mechanisms for allowing its faculty members to participate in its governance, the university historically had no institution permitting its faculty to participate in the governance of the university as a whole. Thus, it lacked a deliberative body that the university administration might consult to obtain the "university faculty's view" on important issues or from which to elect "university faculty representatives" for important committees, such as those conducting searches for a new president or reviewing the university's annual budget. Conversely, the faculty lacked a means to express its views on universitywide issues and concerns.

In 2015, David Harris, the Tufts provost and chief academic officer, established a Faculty Governance Working Group consisting of two members from each of Tufts' eight principal schools to explore ways of strengthening faculty governance at the university. My school, the Fletcher School of Law and Diplomacy, selected me as one of its representatives. In persuading me to accept the assignment, the school's acting dean said, "You're a lawyer. They are probably going to need a lawyer."

After a short introductory meeting in May at the end of the 2014–2015 academic year, the process envisioned by the provost got fully underway in late August 2015 when 16 potential institution builders from Tufts' eight schools convened in an all-day retreat to understand their mission and to explore how they would go about improving faculty governess at the university. Both Tufts President Anthony Monaco and Provost Harris attended the retreat and spoke on the importance of faculty governance, while assuring the working group members of their complete support of the activities that the working group would undertake. It was an effective way to launch an exercise in institution building. The words of the president and the provost were encouraging, and the free lunch was a useful first step in team building among faculty who had little connection with one another before that.

The working group decided to meet every two weeks, beginning at 8 am, and to rotate meetings among the three campuses. Like many institution builders, the group began its work by looking at existing appropriate models and precedents that might guide its work. Its first task was, therefore, to examine the institutions of faculty governance at universities, like Duke, Northwestern, and Georgetown, institutions comparable to Tufts, with strong schools of arts and sciences and an array of distinguished professional schools. Within a short time, it became clear that all these other universities had a governance institution that Tufts lacked: a university faculty senate, a body elected by faculty from throughout the university with authority to decide or advise on universitywide issues. The working group therefore decided to recommend to the university authorities that they create a faculty senate at Tufts, and the group quickly set about the task of designing one. At the same time, they also decided that the working group needed a chair to guide that process, so they asked me to assume that role.

To provide a framework for designing a faculty senate that would meet the needs and circumstances of Tufts University, I prepared a seven-point list of the principal issues that all the faculty senate regulations at other universities seemed to cover: (I) establishment; (II) statement of purposes; (III) senate membership; (IV) senate powers and responsibilities; (V) senate officers and committees; (VI) senate meetings and decision making; and (VII) senate bylaw amendments. The list would serve two important institution-building functions. First, it became the basic agenda for the working group's discussions over the next six months as it considered the details of a faculty senate for Tufts. Second, it also became the structure for the bylaw drafted by the working group and eventually adopted by the Tufts University trustees authorizing the creation of a university faculty senate. I had strongly suggested to the working group that our report of recommendations to the provost should include a draft trustee bylaw creating the faculty senate for adoption by the Board of Trustees, the organ of university governance in which the law vested full power to run the university. I felt a trustee bylaw would give the institution needed stability and sense of permanence. Any future president or provost discontent with a future faculty senate would not be able to make changes unilaterally but would have to secure another bylaw decision from the trustees to abolish or curtail it.

After each working group's biweekly meeting, I drafted a summary of the discussion on the agenda item in a language appropriate for a formal bylaw and then sent it to the working group members for comments and corrections. I would then incorporate their suggested corrections and send the new draft to the group before the next meeting. Using this "single-text procedure," the draft bylaw grew in length and clarity as the working group's discussions progressed. Both the discussion framework and the single-text procedure proved to be useful institution-building tools.

Generally, the working group resolved most issues by consensus. The only issue that encountered significant disagreement was the number of senate representatives to which each school would be entitled, an issue complicated by two factors—the significant academic and cultural differences among the Tufts schools and the variations among them on the standards for determining which members of a school's instructional staffs could be considered "full time." After exploring and discarding the adoption of the "U.S. Senate" model, whereby each school would have an equal number of representatives, and the "U.S. House of Representative Model," whereby the number of school senate members would be strictly in proportion to its number of full-time faculty members, the working group agreed on a formula that roughly reflected the faculty size but gave the smallest schools a minimum number of representatives. Thus, the School of Arts and Sciences, with the university's largest full-time faculty, received seven representatives and the medical school, because of its sizable clinical faculty, received five. The other schools gained three representatives each, except for the School of Biomedical Sciences, which received only two because of its small faculty size. In total, the Tufts faculty consisted of 29 representatives from the university's eight schools.

The working group did not operate in a vacuum. It kept in constant communication with the university administration. The associate provost attended all its meetings, and as working group chair, I met regularly with the provost to update him on the developments. Individual working group members briefed their school's faculty and administration as deliberations progressed. In February 2016, the working group submitted a preliminary report with recommendations to the provost, and after receiving his observations, prepared an interim report, which the provost's council, consisting of school deans and senior university administrators, considered and commented upon. This step in the consultative process led to a revised interim report with draft bylaws, completed in March, for use by individual working group members in consulting the faculties of their individual faculties.

While this consultation process yielded general support for a faculty senate at Tufts, it also revealed suspicion, if not outright resistance, among a few senior administrators, who seemed to fear that a senate would either usurp certain of their functions or become a permanent adversary of the administration. Some were not convinced that it would improve governance at Tufts. One asked me at the beginning of our meeting, "why are you wasting your time with a faculty senate?"

Ultimately, the working group was able to satisfy those concerns and convince senior administrators that a faculty senate at Tufts would help them to communicate and connect with the faculty and, in the end, help university administrators to do their jobs. After receiving feedback from various sources around the university including the president's senior staff, legal counsel, and the secretary of the corporation, the working group submitted a final report to the provost on October 17, 2016, with a draft set of bylaws to establish the Tufts faculty senate by decision of the University Board of Trustees. The trustees adopted the bylaw establishing the senate on November 5, 2016.

After the subsequent elections of the senate representatives in each of Tufts' eight schools, the Tufts faculty senate held its first meeting on April 25, 2017. Building a new institution of democratic governance for the university was furthered in the senate's first year with the creation of five standing committees to carry out basic senate functions: nominations, faculty affairs, research and scholarship, and budget planning and development, in addition to the Senate Executive Committee—to undertake the detailed work of enabling the senate to give useful and meaningful advice on a wide range of topics from recommending faculty colleagues for university appointments to advising on employee health benefits and grievance procedures. In addition, at the first meeting, the senate elected me as its first president, a position I held for a year. By 2024, after seven years of existence, the faculty senate had become an important institution of faculty governance at Tufts University.

Institution Builders' Preliminary Strategies and Tactics

This chapter's discussion of the nature and function of institutions, accompanied by the case study of the Tufts faculty senate, reveals three preliminary strategies that institution builders should consider as they begin their work:

1. The Tufts University faculty senate is a story of institution building from the bottom up—of designing and putting in place an institution by the people whom it was to serve and who were eventually to run and benefit from it. In theory, the university could have chosen an alternative approach: building the faculty senate from the top

down by entrusting its design, development, and enactment entirely to the Tufts University administration. Such an approach would have delegitimated the faculty senate from the outset. Self-interest drives human actions. The faculty would have perceived a faculty senate designed and implemented entirely by the administration as advancing administrative interests, not those of the faculty. The result would have been to delegitimate the decisions of the senate and the institution itself. Few faculty would have any interest in serving as faculty senators and in devoting their time and talents to a faculty senate that emanates from the university administration. To avoid a similar result, institution builders should take care to involve meaningfully the intended institution's operators and beneficiaries in the development and design of the institutions that they are seeking to build.

2. The broad acceptance of the faculty senate within the Tufts University community was due in part to the extensive consultation in which its builders engaged while the institution was in development. Another lesson from the case is that institution builders should consult broadly and early with all persons who may be affected in some way by the intended institution, even though they may not be its intended beneficiaries.

3. Institution building requires effective leadership. The people charged with building an institution should agree on a leader early in the process.

CHAPTER 2

Institution Builders

Institutions do not just spring to life the way Athena sprang from the head of Zeus. They are the product of the work of institution builders, individuals who bring certain indispensable skills and assets to the process of institution building. One may define an institution builder as *a person who seeks in some way to change the existing institutional framework out of a belief that such change will advance that person's interests in some way.* In his scholarship on institutions, Douglass C. North does not use the term "institution builder" but instead states that "… [t]he agent of change is the individual entrepreneur responding to the incentives embodied in the institutional framework."* Although the individual entrepreneur is North's hero in the institutional drama, I have chosen not to use the term "entrepreneur" because it has so many connotations from a multitude of contexts. The term "institution builder" in my judgment is much clearer and functionally specific for the purposes of this book than is the label "entrepreneur."

Sometimes, institution builders are applauded for their efforts. At other times, their contributions go unnoticed. At still other times, they are condemned and punished for their efforts at social change that the institutions they foster will bring. Despite the public reaction that they may engender, one can't talk about institutions without considering the people who make them possible.

The Qualities of Institution Builders

All 16 members of the Tufts working group on faculty governance were institution builders. For nearly 18 months, they dedicated themselves

---

* D.C. North. 1990. *Institutions, Institutional Change, and Economic Performance* 83 (Cambridge University Press). Elsewhere in the same book, on p. 8, North wrote: "Incremental change comes from the perceptions of the entrepreneurs in political and economic organization that they could do better by altering the existing institutional framework at some margin."

steadfastly to creating a permanent institution that would serve the university community for years to come, not out of a desire for personal profit (in fact, there was none to be had) but out of a drive to make Tufts University a better place. A highly diverse group of men and women, specialized in many different areas of knowledge, with a wide range of personalities and individual idiosyncrasies, they all shared a strong commitment to a common goal and were willing to devote their time and effort to achieving it. It is said that people engage in institution building for one of two reasons: mission or money. The 16 members of the Tufts working group joined it out of a deep sense of mission.

It is important to recognize that "institution building" and "team building," a term favored by many corporate leaders to describe what they do, are not the same thing. The purpose of team building is to integrate various individuals into an effectively functioning organization during a given period to achieve specific goals, such as winning baseball games or producing microchips. Institution builders, on the other hand, seek more permanent, long-lasting goals, for example, the end of tribal conflict, the attainment of economic prosperity, or the eradication of disease. Moreover, while leaders as team builders have a time perspective that is usually limited to their terms as leaders, institution builders normally have a time perspective that goes beyond their departure from the scene. One may say that failures in the corporate world sometimes result from leaders who, while perhaps serving as adequate team builders, did not act as effective institution builders for their corporations. Business schools and executive training programs would do well to teach budding corporate CEOs to see themselves as "institution builders" and to manage their enterprises accordingly. This book may help in that effort.

During my summer vacations from college, I worked on a four-person crew that built new sidewalks around the public schools of Niagara Falls, New York, my hometown, which at that time had 100,000 inhabitants. The work tended to follow a basic rhythm. On Monday, we would arrive at school and break up and cart away all or a part of the old sidewalk. Tuesday and Wednesday were usually devoted to leveling the site and installing wooden frames to hold the wet concrete for the new sidewalk. On Thursday, the concrete truck arrived to pour the concrete while the crew worked to shovel and rake it into place within the frames. By Friday, the concrete had hardened, so we would remove the frames and generally groom the site.

The work was hard, but I got a certain satisfaction from it. One day, the job supervisor arrived in his pickup truck and sat in his cab, watching me break up an old sidewalk with a sledgehammer. After a few minutes, he commented memorably as he threw his truck into gear to move on to check on another crew, "When you get to be a lawyer, you can always say you worked for a living." Whenever we had finished a sidewalk and were preparing to move on to another school, I always looked at the new cement sidewalk with satisfaction and a little pride. Here was something we had built that many people would use for a very long time. In its own small way, a sidewalk was an instrument of social order in that it sought to control how and where people might enter the building. *Order*, *social utility*, and *durability*, the goals reflected in my sentiments as I surveyed our work, are precisely the goals that drive many institution builders as they carry out their craft. The same goals have motivated me throughout my career as an institution builder.

Institution Builders in History

The term "institution builder" is often associated with famous leaders who effected desirable change in their countries—leaders like Alexander Hamilton, who as U.S. Secretary of the Treasury laid the foundation for a new country's financial system, and Mother Teresa (born Anjezë Gonxhe Bojaxhiu), an Albanian nun, who built a far-reaching complex of charitable institutions in India and elsewhere to care for the poor and the sick. But the fame and charisma of a Hamilton or a Mother Teresa are not essential for an effective institution builder. What is essential is a strong commitment to the process of institution building, a strategy for its attainment, and a skill in detecting and negotiating the challenges encountered along the way. Of course, Hamilton and Mother Theresa had these attributes as well.

Institution builders are not necessarily the inventors or founders of the institutions they build. Many institution builders have made important social contributions by expanding or transforming existing institutions. In fact, such transformational institution builders often arrive on the scene when an existing institution's effectiveness or very existence is threatened by changing circumstances. John Marshall, the fourth Supreme Court Chief Justice of the United States, was not only a highly effective judicial leader but also an astute institution builder. The Supreme Court in 1801, when Marshall was appointed chief justice by President John Adams, was not the same institution that it was in 1835 when Marshall died while in office. In fact, the U.S. constitutional system still bears the strong imprint of his work, leading one of his biographers to call Marshall "definer of a nation."[1]

A revolutionary war veteran with a stellar career as a state legislator, lawyer, diplomat, member of Congress, and Secretary of State, Marshall had a firm belief in the importance of a strong central government for the future of the country and assumed a definite mission to make the judiciary an effective and coequal instrument of that government. That development would begin with Marshall convincing his colleagues on the court to function as an institution, rather than as six individual justices. Before Marshall's arrival at the court, its six justices wrote separate opinions in each case they decided. Marshal viewed this practice as limiting the court's strength and prestige. In a feat of judicial leadership with far-reaching consequences, he persuaded the other justices that speaking with one voice would increase the court's institutional strength and influence. For each case, he urged them to write just one opinion embodying their decision. In his first three years on the court, Marshall participated in 42 cases. He wrote all the decisions and all of them were unanimous. Later, when President James Madison appointed Joseph Story to the Supreme Court in 1811, he assured a dubious Thomas Jefferson that Story would remain faithful to Jeffersonian principles. Within a short time, Story had become Marshall's strongest supporter, while expressing the worry that Jefferson's continuing influence "...would destroy the government of his country."[2]

As a successful former diplomat and politician, Marshall understood the importance of relationships and how to craft them. A skilled and experienced negotiator, he effectively relied on negotiation to lead the court. One of the reasons that he was able to lead the other Supreme Court Justices to unanimous decisions on key constitutional questions that laid the foundation for the American republic was the fact that he arranged for them all to live together in the same Washington boarding

house where they shared meals together, often over a bottle of claret sup-
plied by Marshall, and discussed their cases, the politics of the day, and
life itself.[3] What Marshall achieved through this arrangement was to build
strong working relations with and among his colleagues that would enable
him to lead and to build the Supreme Court as one of the most effective
chief justices in the history of the United States. Marshall understood that
institution builders need to negotiate to achieve their goals.

In his 34 years as chief justice, John Marshall presided over more than
1,000 cases with fewer than a dozen dissents, surely a remarkable feat of
judicial leadership. He also persuaded his judicial colleagues that speaking with one voice would increase the court's institutional strength and
influence. The Marshall court would lay the foundation of constitutional
government in the United States, including the supremacy of the con-
stitution and the power of the courts to refuse enforcement of laws and
regulations that violated it. It also defined the role of the chief justice,
principles which have lasted until the present day. He was assuredly a
powerful institution builder from whom present-day institution builders
may learn much.

In many searches for new organizational leaders, people entrusted
with the search are often looking for not only a new leader but also an
institution builder who will complete or continue the task of building
their institution. In my own case, when I was appointed as dean of the
School of Law of Southern Methodist University and then six years later
as dean of the Fletcher School of Law and Diplomacy at Tufts University,
the presidents of both universities told me at the time of my appointment, "we are bringing you here to build." Neither man was asking me
to construct buildings. Instead, they were encouraging me to build and
strengthen two essential elements of any academic institution: the faculty
and the student body. My focus in both schools was to recruit talented
scholars to the faculty and to raise scholarship funds to attract bright and
diverse students. I was happy to achieve both goals at the two institutions.

Incremental Institution Builders

Institutions do not always spring from a grand plan as the Tufts Faculty
Senate did. Sometimes, they emerge from a series of independent uncon-
nected actions that at the time did not appear to form an institution.

For example, consider the case of three friends who like to cook and meet monthly to try out new recipes. After two years of receiving enthusiastic receptions for this cooking from their families and friends, they decide to self-publish a book of their recipes and, after the book achieved great success in the market, set up a small school to teach novices how to cook like chefs. Their pleasant past time had evolved into an institution. An interesting question is: At what point did their activities morph into an institution? Similarly, a group of parents, unhappy with the local primary school for their children, after making individual complaints to the school leadership, banded together to pressure the town board of education to make improvements in the school and provide additional needed resources. Receiving only polite noncommittal responses, the parents ultimately formed a charter school under state law. Here was another example of incremental institution building.

Several years ago, I unintentionally became involved in what became an unintended process of institution building. Shortly after I arrived at the Fletcher School in 1986 to take up the deanship, I met Professor Jeffrey Z. Rubin, a senior member of the Tufts Psychology Department and a noted expert on negotiation. At that time, Jeff was also serving as Deputy Director of the Program on Negotiation (PON) at Harvard Law School, an interuniversity consortium of Harvard, MIT, and Tufts. Jeff invited me to participate in PON activities and to write columns in its review, *Negotiation Journal.* Since I had used negotiation in teaching international business transactions at Southern Methodist Law School, where I had been dean, I was grateful for the offer. As a result, we became close friends and colleagues.

In the fall of 1987, Tufts President Jean Mayer, learning of our collaboration, asked Jeff and me to prepare a university-level model syllabus for teaching negotiation and dispute resolution and to present it at an international conference of university presidents that he was planning to host the following summer at the Tufts campus in Talloires, France. His goal was to encourage universities in the United States and abroad to offer courses on negotiation and conflict resolution, which some university leaders resisted since they did not consider such courses "academic."

The syllabus and reading list that we ultimately developed, a document of over 100 pages, emphasized skill building and drew heavily on simulations and case studies that focused on international negotiations and conflicts. At the Talloires conference, our syllabus was well received by university leaders from around the world, who said they hoped to encourage a similar course at their home universities. (The vice chancellor of an Indian university was an exception. Doubting the utility of such a course for third-world countries, he stated that "A negotiation between the weak and strong is like a conversation between the lamb and the lion: the lamb always gets eaten," a statement that later led us to write a piece entitled "How Should the Lamb Negotiate with the Lion?")

After Jeff and I completed our presentation at the conference, we went for a walk on the mountain above Talloires. When I asked him what we should do next, he replied, "Let's teach our course at Fletcher," pointing out that the Fletcher School curriculum had no course on negotiation. When I told him that I was not sure that the Fletcher budget had sufficient funds to hire him, he responded, "Let's do it as an overload." And that was exactly what we did, offering the course for the first time in the fall of 1988. We had originally expected a class of 15 students. On the first day that we offered the course, we found over 50 students had signed up, so we had to move the class to a larger classroom in another building on the Tufts campus. From that moment, the course on negotiation and conflict resolution became a permanent and popular feature of the Fletcher curriculum. Jeff was a dynamic and engaging teacher and also an effective institution builder.

Within a year or two, I found the money to buy half of Jeff's time from the Psychology Department and appoint him a professor at the Fletcher School. Shortly thereafter, he developed and taught a course on international mediation and began to supervise PhD students in negotiation. We continued to teach the negotiation course jointly and even developed and taught an executive program on international business negotiation for a few years. Ultimately, we formed the Fletcher Program on Negotiation and Dispute Resolution. Our efforts had morphed into an institution. We were incremental institution builders.

In June 1995, while I was on sabbatical leave in England, Jeff tragically died in a mountain climbing accident in Maine. On my return to Fletcher in January 1996, I continued to teach the negotiation course alone for a time, in addition to my law courses, but student demand was so great that the school decided to undertake a search for a full-time professor of negotiation. Ultimately, it hired Eileen Babbitt as its first full-time professor of negotiation and conflict resolution in the school's history. She was still with us in 2023. In the face of increasing student demand, the school over the years added other instructors in negotiation to its faculty so that, by 2023 the Fletcher School Program on Negotiation and Conflict had a faculty of four-time professors. I think it is true to say that out of Rubin's and my walk on the mountain, a robust new institution evolved, the Program on Negotiation and Conflict Resolution.

Conclusion: Tools for Building an Institution-Building Team

Institution builders work most effectively in teams. Indeed, it is hard to conceive of an institution that has not emerged from a team effort. Like a sports team manager or a head coach, an individual seeking to build an institution has an early challenge in putting together a team to construct the desired institution. The challenge for the institution builder is twofold: to find the right people and then to convince them to join the institution-building team. In scouting for potential team members, institution builders may look for people with the following qualities:

1. A skill that is useful in building the desired institution.
2. A strong belief in the importance of team's mission.
3. An ability to plan and execute long-term projects.
4. An understanding of the proposed institution's subject matter.
5. An ability to negotiate effectively with other people.
6. A team player.

Carrying out the search may become the team leader's task or fall to an unofficial "scout" that the team leader has asked to help with the search. Once a potential team member has been identified, the team leader must then negotiate an agreement with that individual to join the team. That negotiation begins by understanding the candidate's interests and then demonstrating how the institution-building project relates to those interests. Equally important, to close the deal, the team leader may have to adjust the terms of the candidate's participation on such matters as starting date, daily hours of work, and time-off for personal matters.

CHAPTER 3

The Elements of Negotiating Institutions

Institution builders must *negotiate* to achieve their goals. Indeed, they do so to such an extent that one may say that institution building is essentially a process of negotiation and that institution builders must be effective negotiators if they are to succeed in building anything. The purpose of this chapter is to examine some basic negotiation concepts.

Negotiating Positions and Interests

Negotiation can be defined as "a process of communication by which two or more people seek to advance their individual interests by agreeing on a desired course of action."[1] As the definition indicates, interests of the parties are key factors in driving any negotiation. What are interests? They are *not*, as one executive suggested to me, "my hobbies or what I like to do on the weekends." Simply put, your interests are what are important to you. In any negotiation, it is critical to understand the other side's interests as well as your own. It is also important to distinguish parties' *interests* from their *positions* in a negotiation. Parties' positions are their stated demands, which may or may not reflect their unstated interests beneath those positions. When parties' stated positions are far apart, progress toward a settlement of their differences may begin only when the parties understand and discuss their previously unstated underlying interests.

A case that illustrates the importance of understanding parties' interests involved a negotiation between two daughters of a recently deceased wealthy man whose last will and testament directed that "all my personal property shall be shared equally by two daughters." The discussions between the two daughters concerning the division of their father's personal property went smoothly and congenially, until it came to the old man's ring. He had worn a large diamond ring for most of his life, and both daughters wanted it. Both asserted identical negotiating positions: "I want the ring." Following the patterns of many negotiations, each daughter sought to justify her position by relying on a norm or principle. One daughter pointed out that she had taken care of their father in his old age and should rightfully have the ring, whereas the other daughter claimed that her father had promised the ring to her years before so she should have it. Relations between the two women became tense. Finally, in frustration, one daughter asked the other a key question: "Why do you want the ring?" The question was key because its purpose was to determine her sister's interests that lay beneath her stated negotiating position. The reply to the question was: "I want the ring because it has a lovely diamond. I thought I would remove the diamond and make a pendant from it." Startled, the other daughter responded," That's not why I want the ring. I want it as a memento of our father."

The daughters' interests underlying their initial positions had now become clear. One daughter's interest was in having the ring's diamond, whereas the other's interest was the ring's sentimental value. When the two daughters realized that their interests, while different, were not necessarily incompatible, they began to explore mutually acceptable solutions to the ring problem. Finally, the daughter whose interest in the ring was sentimental proposed that her sister take the ring to a jeweler, have the diamond replaced with the first daughter's birthstone, keep the diamond, pay the jeweler's fee for the conversion, and return the altered ring to the first daughter. The second daughter immediately accepted the offer. It was only by determining the interests that underlay their stated positions that the two women were able to overcome what appeared to be an insurmountable barrier at the start of the negotiations.

Internal and External Negotiations

Negotiation takes place at two levels in the institution-building process: (1) internal negotiations within the group of institution builders about how the institution-building process should take place; and (2) external negotiations between the institution builders and outside persons and organizations to gain the resources and permissions necessary to build the institution. The two types of negotiation may be conceptually separate, but in practice they are often connected. For example, if you are leading the building of an international environmental institution to protect whales and other sea mammals, you will have to manage internal negotiations with your embryonic staff on a research program, as well as external negotiations with external funders over the kinds and conditions of research that your institution may undertake with their money. Once the institution's research is under way, you may find that your staff is conducting a research program not strictly covered by the external grant, a situation that will require you to renegotiate grant conditions or staff research guidelines or both.

Bilateral and Multilateral Negotiations

People often view negotiations as hostile interactions with another person; however, hostility is not a required element for a negotiation. Any interaction, friendly or antagonistic, with another person that meets the above definition is a negotiation. The conversation that Jeff Rubin and I had on the mountain above Talloires, France, to figure out what we were going to do with our international negotiation syllabus was a negotiation. Stripped of verbiage, our negotiation was as follows:

> JWS: "What should we do with our syllabus?" (statement of the issue)
> JZR: "Let's teach it at Fletcher." (offer)
> JWS: "No money in the budget for that." (rejection)
> JZR: "Let's do it as an overload." (counteroffer)
> JWS: OK. (agreement)

My negotiation with Jeff Rubin was basically a simple interaction, a two-sided communication between two parties who knew each other well and whose individual interests were very similar. Many, if not most, negotiations required of institution builders are not simple *bilateral* affairs, but, like the negotiations that took place among the 16-member Tufts University Faculty Governance Working Group, are *multilateral* interactions.

A "party" to a negotiation is not only someone who participates in the discussions but also someone whose interests are at stake and whose consent is necessary for any agreement to take place. International diplomacy has traditionally distinguished between *bilateral*—two-sided—negotiations and meetings on the one hand and *multilateral*—more than two sides—on the other. In a bilateral negotiation, there are only two parties; in a multilateral negotiation, there are more than two. The reason for this distinction lies not just in the differing number of parties but also in the consequences that the number of parties has on the negotiation process. Essentially, a multilateral negotiation differs from a bilateral negotiation in two important respects: complexity and power dynamics.

First, the inclusion of more parties in a negotiation complicates the process because it introduces increased issues and interests that must be accommodated to reach an agreement. For example, a bilateral trade negotiation between the United States and Mexico, while not simple, only needs to accommodate the interests and issues of the two countries concerned. On the other hand, a multilateral negotiation among the countries of the world to create a global trade regime would have to deal with countless interests and concerns of nearly 150 nations, a process that took place during the Uruguay Round of trade negotiations, which lasted eight years, from 1986 to 1994. Similarly, a conversation between you and your spouse about where to go to dinner is usually a simple bilateral negotiation that you can usually complete quickly. A discussion on the same topic at a family reunion among you, your spouse, your three sisters, and their spouses, a group that includes a vegan, a person on a weight-loss regime, another worried about his high cholesterol, and yet another on a tight budget, will rapidly develop into a multilateral negotiation whose complexity approaches that of the Uruguay Round. Similarly, institution builders seeking to establish a new charter school will usually bring to the table a diverse set of interests and desires about the school's philosophy, teaching staff, location, architecture, and student body size, a package that will require a sophisticated negotiated resolution.

A multilateral negotiation's second major difference resides in the power dynamic that takes place in multilateral negotiations because of the ability of the parties to form coalitions and alliances as mechanisms to influence a desired result. In a strictly bilateral negotiation with the United

States, Mexico is alone in facing its northern neighbor. In a multilateral negotiation, such as the Uruguay Round, Mexico can build coalitions with countries having similar interests and try to use those coalitions to influence the results of the negotiation in desired ways. A similar dynamic takes place in the decision-making process of any group, whether it is a company, local government, civic organization, or set of individuals. Generally, parties engaged in such efforts have one of two purposes: (1) to create a "winning coalition" that will lead to the adoption of a decision in their favor or (2) to create a "blocking coalition" to prevent the adoption of a decision that is against their interests.

It is through coalition building that a country, organization, or individual can increase its power in a multilateral negotiation, something that is impossible in a strictly bilateral negotiation, since there is no other party with which to build a coalition. For example, developing countries often build coalitions in multilateral conferences to block decisions favored by developed countries and to push for the adoption of decisions that favor the interests of the developing world. Similarly, you may find that in choosing a restaurant for dinner at your family reunion, the vegan, the weight-loss guy, and the low-cholesterol maniac will build an effective blocking coalition to stop any move toward that great steak house you remember from your youth. They may even succeed in constructing a winning coalition, forcing you to spend the evening in a vegetarian restaurant. The same phenomenon may take place among parents seeking to establish a charter school who cannot agree on its academic focus and philosophy. Ultimately, coalitions may develop between those who want a school strongly devoted to the arts and those who seek one with a strong athletic program, forcing parents who demand a heavily science program to compromise.

If you believe you are in the dominant position in a negotiation, a bilateral, one-to-one process allows you to apply your power without restrictions. A multilateral negotiation, on the other hand, may dilute your power and reduce your influence. It is for this reason that in international diplomacy a country's preference for a bilateral or multilateral setting in which to negotiate depends largely on that country's perception of how a particular setting will affect its negotiating power, that is, its ability to influence the decisions of another country with which it is concerned.

For this reason, the United States and other powerful countries prefer to conduct important diplomatic issues on a bilateral basis with other countries individually while small developing countries seek to hold discussions on those same issues in multilateral meetings and conferences that enable them to form coalitions and alliances with governments having similar interests, and thus increase their influence. The U.S. government has been successful in signing many bilateral investment treaties with developing countries, while multilateral efforts to achieve a global treaty on investment have failed. It is only when a powerful country cannot obtain what it wants from bilateral discussions that it turns to multilateral efforts. For example, the United States' perceived inability to persuade Iraq through bilateral negotiations to evacuate Kuwait led it to build a coalition for war through a series of multilateral negotiations in 1991.

There may be times when it will be advantageous to try to convert a bilateral negotiation in which you are involved into multilateral talks by including one or more other people as parties to the conversation. For example, if you and your spouse are trying to decide where to go on vacation in the summer and your spouse is once again pushing to go to an uncle's decrepit lake house in the boring north woods (a place where the family went last summer), it may be a good idea to suggest that your two teenage children, who don't like the lake house any more than you do, get in on the conversation. Similarly, if your department head is insisting on launching a project that you think will be a disaster, try to convert the conversation into a multilateral negotiation by involving your top technical folks in the decision-making process. In both instances, you *multilateralize* what began as a bilateral negotiation. On the other hand, there may be instances when *bilateralizing* a multilateral conversation may help to achieve a solution. For example, suppose you are chairing a staff meeting of institution builders to decide on a new strategic initiative and the group discussion is going in a dozen direct directions and approaching a state of chaos. You might consider selecting two people who represent dominant, but differing views within the group and ask them to meet together and negotiate a solution for presentation to the group.[2]

Third persons become involved in many negotiations without actually being parties. Diplomacy is filled with examples where other individuals, organizations, and countries participated in negotiations or disputes between other countries and groups to help them reach agreement and settle their conflicts. Thus, Jimmy Carter mediated the dispute between Egypt and Israel, leading to their peace treaty of 1979. Former senator George Mitchell spent two years brokering a settlement in 1999 between Catholics and Protestants in Northern Ireland, ending 30 years of a bloody and destructive civil war. And the late Richard Holbrooke, as U.S. assistant secretary of state, engineered a settlement among the warring parties in Bosnia to end the Balkan war, resulting in the Dayton Peace Accords of 1995. Each of these men operated in different ways to achieve the results they did. Each also received significant public acclaim for resolving disputes that seemed intractable at the time. In cases in which institution builders disagree on how to proceed, thereby threatening the institution-building process with failure, the intervention of an outsider as mediator or advisor may help the group find a solution to their dilemma.

The Importance of Leadership

The success of any multilateral negotiation among institution builders requires someone to lead the process. Otherwise, the negotiation will drone on interminably. If you have a leadership position with the group, what is the best way to carry out your role to help the group agree on a vision for its task? The case of Goldman Sachs' multiyear negotiation to determine a new vision for itself in a new era is instructive.

Negotiating a Vision for Goldman Sachs

Goldman Sachs is a well-established financial institution whose roots go back to the 19th century. At the end of the 20th century, its partners were not trying to create a new institution but rather to modernize an established institution to function in the 21st century. They were therefore institution builders.

In the rapidly changing world of international finance at the end of the 20th century, the leaders at Goldman Sachs, a venerable investment banking partnership, faced the challenge of negotiating a vision for the bank's role in the 21st century among its partners, a task that would require more than a decade of discussions, carefully orchestrated by firm leaders, to negotiate its transformation into a publicly-traded corporation.

In 1986, investment bank Goldman Sachs was a $38 billion business owned by more than 100 active and retired partners. While the partnership structure had insulated the company from the vicissitudes of the stock market and given it a strong culture of teamwork, it had some significant disadvantages, of which the two most significant were its inability to grow by making acquisitions with stock and its unstable capital base because whenever partners left the partnership, they took their capital with them. Because of these factors, the firm's nine-person management committee recommended that Goldman Sachs become a corporation and sell its shares to the public. Over a weekend in December 1986, all Goldman partners met to consider this new vision. Rather than presenting a *fait accompli*, Goldman's leadership stayed faithful to the firm's ingrained teamwork culture during the two-day retreat. The partners debated the proposal at length and with high emotion, but the meeting ended with no decision. Goldman Sachs therefore remained a partnership.

After 10 years, the partners of Goldman Sachs once again considered a proposal to become a publicly traded corporation. This time, a special committee prepared an exhaustively detailed proposal for an initial public offering (IPO), and the firm leaders actively lobbied partners to support it. Once again, a weekend partnership meeting was held to consider the firm's future. When it became clear to the executive committee that the partners did not want to change the firm, the committee withdrew the IPO proposal.

Two years later, in 1998, the firm's leadership established a subcommittee to plot the firm's strategy in a rapidly changing global financial environment. Ultimately, the committee recommended a five-year program of aggressive growth that included going public, and the firm's two cochairmen then engaged in one-on-one conversations with nearly all the firm's 190 partners to persuade them to accept the recommendation. In June 1998, for yet a third time, the partners of Goldman Sachs met in a weekend retreat. This time, the partners voted to sell the firm's shares to the public. After 12 years of meetings and discussions, the leadership of Goldman Sachs finally succeeded in negotiating a multilateral vision to carry the firm into the 21st century.

Why did Goldman Sachs succeed in going public in 1998 when the proposal to do so had died two times before? And why did it take so long? Could other leaders have achieved the same result in less time? Would the prototypical, dynamic corporate CEO of the time—a Jack Welch, a Louis Gerstner, or a Sandy Weill—have done a more effective job of leading Goldman Sachs to a new strategic vision than the Goldman leadership? The answer to that question is: almost certainly not. The partners of Goldman Sachs, who, unlike the employees, owned the firm, had the power to say "no" to any proposal, to remove from leadership anyone who they felt threatened their interests, and to replace that person with someone who better served them. In the Goldman Sachs' situation, it was not vision and charisma that would lead the partners, but an understanding of the partners' interests and an ability to convince them that a needed new direction advanced those interests. The strategic change at Goldman Sachs was an example of interest-based, institution building of the highest order. Adopting a new vision required Goldman's leadership to painstakingly forge a coalition among the partners they led.[3]

Conclusion: Tools for Negotiating Institution Building

Although the Goldman Sachs' case is special, in many ways, it does illustrate some basic principles for negotiating the process of institution building. Here are a few:

1. *Determine a direction for the group by structuring and conducting a strategic conversation.* For Goldman Sachs, determining a new direction for the firm was the product of a conversation that took 13 years. For institution building, finding a strategic direction is also the product of a conversation. The basic task of the group's leadership is to structure and conduct that conversation, rather than to try to impose a new vision from the top. While few organizations will require 13 years to find their way as Goldman did, it is important to realize that conducting a strategic conversation about organizational direction can be time consuming and often frustrating.

2. *Develop a fair process for conducting the conversation about direction.*
   If you, as the group's leader, think you have a clear vision of the
   institution's future and a distinct sense of the best direction to follow,
   resist the temptation to try to impose it on the others in the institution-building team. As Machiavelli noted over 500 years ago, the
   dangers for a leader in trying to impose a new order is that you will
   make enemies of those who benefited from the old order and gain
   only lukewarm support from those who stand to benefit from the
   new. In the end, your enemies may prevent you from imposing your
   new order, and even if you overcome them, they will remain opponents as you go about the process of implementing it. This does not
   mean, of course, that you abandon any hope of moving the group in
   a more productive direction. Rather, it means that you need to find
   and develop a process that will enable its members to participate in
   determining new directions. In the Goldman Sachs' case, the firm
   worked out a definite process of meetings and consultations to help
   the partners arrive at a new strategic direction.

3. *Establish a fair process that includes the opportunity for group members'
   genuine participation in decision making based on acceptable principles
   and standards.* The process by which Goldman Sachs arrived at a
   decision to adopt a new strategic direction was based on the full
   participation of all the partners in the deliberations. All the partners
   had the right to speak, and all were sincerely encouraged to do so.
   They exercised that right throughout the 13 years that the decision
   was under consideration. The goal of the conversation is not merely
   to determine a direction but also to cause the members of the organization to adopt, believe in, and work enthusiastically toward the
   direction that is decided. Ownership of the decision by members
   of the group is a key to success. Ownership is much more likely to
   result if the members played a part in making the decision on direction than if the organization's leaders arrived at their desired decision
   by dominating or short-circuiting the process.

4. *Once you have established a process, use it genuinely to help determine a
   direction for your organization.* Sometimes, leaders put in place a process of consultation that is merely a charade, a means to justify what
   they wanted to do in the first place. People usually come to know

when they are engaged in meaningless activity. Once they realize that they are involved in a purely formal process that has little or no significance, they will also participate in a purely formal way, if at all.

5. *Your most effective tool for institution building is not the order but the right question.* The leadership of Goldman Sachs, after two failed attempts to convince the partners to go public, reframed the question that they were to answer from "Should the firm go public?" to "What should be the firm's strategy in the radically changed financial environment at the end of the 20th century?" This was a question that affected the vital interests of the firm and all its partners. It was a question that was designed to elicit the strong and positive participation of all. Once the firm had answered the basic questions by deciding to be a world-class financial firm, it then had to face the question of finding the resources to compete with much larger competitors. This question, in turn, led the partners to decide on going public, which would give the firm through its publicly traded shares the currency to vastly expand its operations. In leading an effort at institution building, your most effective instrument may be the right question.

CHAPTER 4

The Seven Tasks of Institution Building

Although the world's institutions, from global banks to village courts demonstrate bewildering complexity, the process of building an institution tends to follow a basic pattern regardless of institutional size and where it takes place. The birth of an institution tends to pass through seven developmental stages. Each stage requires a set of tasks that institution builders must accomplish if their institution is to see the light of day. For each task, negotiation is the institution builder's principal tool. Let's look briefly at all seven tasks in this chapter and then examine each one in depth in the seven chapters that follow.

Task #1: Launching the Institution-Building Process

An institution builder's first and essential task is to launch the institution-building process—to bring together people with the appropriate skills, interests, and resources to work on building the needed institution and to generate the impetus causing that work to take place. Depending on the bureaucratic practices in the country concerned, that group may be called a "task force," "board of advisors," "consultative committee," or simply a "working group." Its members may be appointed by a superior authority, such as a corporate CEO, governmental minister, or organizational leader, as was the case of the Tufts University Faculty Governance Working Group, or composed of volunteers recruited by persons leading the effort to build an institution. To accomplish the task in the latter situation, an institution builder may have to negotiate a series of agreements to gain the participation of needed individuals. The role that these individuals play may vary from being mere advisors to the working group's leadership to making decisions affecting the proposed institution and contributing resources to support it. As is the case with any launch, one of the functions of the institution-building process launch is to see whether the idea for a new institution floats or sinks.

Task #2: Negotiating the Institutional Vision

Once convened, the working group will have to agree on a vision for the contemplated institution, particularly its nature and purposes. In most cases, that effort will require a multilateral negotiation to harmonize the various interests of working group members. To aid in this task, the group should study instructive precedents of similar institutions, examine their relevant documents, and consult with people having experience in working for or interacting with such institutions. The results of these deliberations should be embodied in a carefully drafted document, which might take the form of a brief declaration of institutional purpose or a more elaborate mission statement. In whatever form it takes, such a document will guide the institution-building process and inform relevant external bodies, like funding agencies or government departments, of the proposed institution's aims and intentions. At the same time, the working group should be prepared to modify the document as circumstances require.

Task #3: Negotiating the Institutional Plan

An important task in institution building is negotiating a development plan for the proposed institution. That document will cover its structure, personnel, methods of operation, and needed resources. The planning process will serve to educate the task force members about the challenges and opportunities facing the proposed institution and thereby heighten its chances for success. Upon assuming the deanships of the Southern Methodist University Law School and later the Fletcher School of Law and Diplomacy at Tufts University, I launched strategic planning processes involving each school's entire faculty and senior staff. The result not only guided institution building at both institutions but also helped to create a heightened sense of community among the individuals participating in the planning process. Working on a common problem tends to build positive relationships among participants in the activity. It is an important institution-building tool.

Task #4: Negotiating Institutional Resources

All institutions need resources, both human and material, to function. The sources and methods of financing a new institution will depend fundamentally on its nature and the environment in which it will function. For example, resourcing a new governmental organization differs fundamentally from a civic organization. A governmental organization can usually rely to a certain extent on resources from the government's budget. A civic organization, on the other hand, usually has no such assurance. Nonetheless, the task of resourcing an institution in its early days will usually fall on the institution builders involved, requiring them to become persuasive advocates for the institution they are building. In soliciting support from governments or private sources, institution builders should prepare a funding plan for the first few years of the institution's life. They should also be aware that while funders' enthusiasm may be strong at the beginning of an institution's life, that enthusiasm may later wane and result in a reduction of external support. Institution builders often face the challenge of obtaining funding in the early years of an institution's life while being able to show that long-term funding is also a strong possibility. At the same time, it is important to take advantage of whatever enthusiasm exists in the early days of an institution to secure its funding.

Task #5: Negotiating the Institution's Legalization

Whether a contemplated institution is governmental or civic in nature, it is always based in the territory of a particular country and is, therefore, subject to that country's laws, regulations, and governmental authority. As a result, to be sure that a contemplated institution will be allowed to function in that country, an institution builder must oversee the institution's legalization by assuring that it has complied with relevant laws and regulations. To succeed in this task, an institution builder will ordinarily seek the assistance of a lawyer.

The task of legalization has various purposes. Two of the most important are to gain the new institution's legal recognition as an entity separate and apart from the persons who are organizing it and to entitle it to take advantage of various rights and privileges that the governing legal system may grant to such institutions. To attain either of these goals, institution builders must have the special skills for negotiating with governments.

Task #6: Negotiating to Promote the Institution

The tasks considered thus far all relate to the design and construction of institutions. A subsequent task that some, but not all, institution builders may be called upon to undertake is to promote the acceptance of the proposed institution by important individuals and groups, acceptance that is essential if that institution is to become a reality within the society for which it was designed. To gain that necessary acceptance, institution builders will often undertake campaigns of persuasion. To carry out that task, institution builders need to ask two fundamental questions: (1) Who needs to be persuaded? (2) What message will persuade them?

Two groups will be particular targets of persuasion. The first are governmental units whose approval is necessary if the institution is to come into existence and receive assistance. The second are those individuals and organizations who are entitled to use the new institution but may refrain from doing so either because they do not understand it or because they fear its risks.

Task #7: Negotiating Knowledge

Institutions run on knowledge. A vital task for any institution builder is to find and obtain the necessary knowledge for the institution to function. A skilled baseball team manager does not need to know how to throw a fading curve ball, but that manager must know how to find somebody who can throw one and then to commit that person to a contract to play for the team. Similarly, institution builders seeking to establish a charter school, a venture capital firm, or missionary clinic must understand the various areas of knowledge and skills that such institutions need and find ways to secure them for the institutions that they are trying to build.

Obtaining knowledge for the institution is the seventh and final task of institution building—yet another task that requires skillful negotiation by the institution builder.

Institution Builders' Seven Tasks and Leadership

Any effective institution builder's playbook must include strategies and tactics to carry out the following seven tasks of institution building:

1. Negotiating the process launch
2. Negotiating an institutional vision
3. Negotiating an institutional plan
4. Negotiating institutional resources
5. Legalizing the institution
6. Promoting the institution
7. Negotiating knowledge

Within the context of many institution-building scenarios that involve numerous parties, for example, the creation of a charter school or the negotiation of an international corporate joint venture, the effectiveness of institution builders in carrying out any of these tasks will depend on the quality of their leadership. Any multiparty activity without leadership is doomed to failure. For purposes of this book, we can define leadership as "the ability to cause other individuals to act willingly in a desired way for the benefit of the group."[1] That ability is derived basically from leaders' ability to communicate persuasively with other people and negotiate the numerous agreements upon which every institution rests. In the next seven chapters, we will examine each of these institution-building tasks in detail to see how institution builders may negotiate them to build the institutions they are seeking.

CHAPTER 5

Task #1: Launching the Institution-Building Process

An institution builder's first, essential task is to launch the institution-building *process*, the operation that will hopefully lead to the creation of the desired institution. Normally, like organizing a theater production or athletic event, one or more individuals will need to act as *institutional promoters* by bringing together people with the appropriate skills, interests, and resources to work on building the desired institution.

The complexity and duration of launching the building process depends on numerous factors, including the number of people involved, the goals of the contemplated institution, the amount and nature of the resources needed, and the kind of institution that is to be built. The launching process may be divided into two phases: (1) the decision to launch the process of institution building and (2) the implementation of the launching procedure. Tufts University's process leading to the creation of its faculty senate was decided by the university's provost after a few months of informal discussions with various university leaders, but the launching actually took place at the first meeting of the working group, whose members had been appointed by the Tufts school in which they were faculty members. On the other hand, it took 123 nations four years, from 1982 to 1986, merely to launch the Uruguay Round of Trade Negotiations, an institution-building exercise of multilateral negotiations that would last an additional eight years (1986 to 1994) and result in the creation of a new international institution, the World Trade Organization. Based on that experience, one may say that the difficulty, cost, and duration of launching an institution-building process increase in direction proportion to the number of parties involved and the importance of the stakes. First, the number of parties, and therefore the number of interests to accommodate, increases the time necessary to negotiate a process that will satisfy all concerned. Second, the high stakes inherent in a topic like international trade, which has a significant impact on a nation's prosperity, causes governments to be cautious in making commitments and therefore slows the negotiation process considerably.

Accomplishing the launch of an institution-building process requires four elements: (1) one or more institutional promoters, (2) an institution-building team, (3) an agreed agenda or set of goals and other preparatory measures, and (4) a well-planned first meeting.

1. Institutional Promoters

Promoters are important actors in many economies. They identify or develop a business idea and then find the capital and people to convert it into a functioning business operation. Derived from two Latin words, "*pro*" meaning forward and "*movere*" to move, a promoter's basic function is to move forward an idea or activity by finding the people and resources necessary to make it a reality. Promoters are, by their nature, institution builders. They have a strong commitment to an idea that they want to develop, the needed energy and personal resources to expend, the ability to communicate and negotiate effectively with other people, and the willingness to risk failure. They often see the first step in achieving their goals as the orchestration of an institution-building process by recruiting people with the talents and resources to work with them in building the desired institution or enterprise.

To prepare for the recruitment process and generate interest among possible recruits and other supporters, institutional promoters may wish to develop a short policy paper covering at least three topics: (1) problem identification, (2) problem analysis, and (3) possible policy options. The right policy statement is an important institution-building tool.

a) *Problem identification.* At the heart of any effort to build a new institution or repair an old one is a problem that people believe is negatively affecting their lives. These problems range widely from a poorly performing public school to an unprofitable corporate division. A compelling problem identification statement requires significant research, including interviews with people directly affected by the problem.

b) *Problem analysis.* Having identified the problem, the policy paper should next seek to discuss the reasons for the problem. Why is the school performing poorly? Why is the corporate division losing money? To be truly convincing, this part of the policy paper should look in depth at all the forces that shape the problem, not merely those advanced by a particular interest group. For example, if the failing school has been caused by lack of financial support from a town's government as well as weak internal leadership, both causes should be examined.

c) *Possible policy options.* Finally, the paper should suggest possible measures that might be taken to correct the situation. For example, the underperforming school might be transformed into a charter school and the unprofitable corporate division might be sold. At the same time, care should be taken to indicate that the statements in the policy paper are tentative and subject to the definitive findings of the institution-building team that will be appointed. It is important not to preempt or be seen to control the working of the institution-building team. To avoid any suggestion of control by the Tufts University administration, the university's provost wisely did not establish a "Faculty Senate Task Force," which would have indicated a definite goal for the group, but instead designated the institution-building team as "the Working Group on Faculty Governance." That title for the working group made clear that the problem to be studied was faculty governance in the broadest sense. If the creation of a faculty senate was a solution to that problem, it was up to the working group, not the provost, to make that determination. By the label he chose for the working group, the provost was affirming its autonomy.

2. Institution-Building Team

To create an institution-building team having the necessary skills and contacts to do the job, an institutional promoter will have to apply the same level of care as a baseball team manager deciding on a starting lineup for a championship game or a theatrical producer choosing a cast for a new play. Toward that end, the promoter usually will have to negotiate a series of agreements to gain the participation of needed individuals with desired skills like finance, law, accounting, and organizational management. The roles that individual team members may play in the institution-building process may vary from serving as the working group's leader to making decisions on its finances.

But unlike a team manager selecting players for a big game, an institution builder in many cases must also take account of and assure the representation of the people who will be affected by the contemplated institution. Thus, in launching a charter school, the institution-building team should include strong representation of parents whose children will attend the school. In fact, that representation might be assured by organizing an election of people to represent the community that the new charter school will serve. In the case of Tufts University's efforts to build a faculty senate, all members of the Faculty Governance Working Group, which designed and implemented the senate, were chosen by the school faculties where they taught. This selection process for the working group members was designed to give its eventual decisions legitimacy in the eyes of the Tufts University faculty, the group that the faculty senate was to serve.

In general, the basic techniques of appointing members of an institution-building team consist of one of four general procedures:

i) Election, whereby the members of the institution-building team are elected by a vote of an appropriate body or group

ii) Shuttle diplomacy, whereby the institutional promoter negotiates the participation individually of potential task force members, somewhat the way Henry Kissinger did to broker a cease-fire between Israel and Egypt after the six-day war in 1974

iii) Bandwagoning, whereby the institutional leader sends out a more or less public call for volunteers and then negotiates their roles when individuals respond positively to the invitation

iv) Negotiations under the protection of a patron, whereby the institution builder relies on the power and prestige of an influential person or institution to gain task force members. Numerous factors may influence these negotiations, not the least of which is whether the contemplated institution is governmental or civic in nature.

As in any negotiation, it is important to understand the interests of the parties participating or affected by the process. As indicated earlier, in the context of a negotiation, the parties' interests are what are important to them. Scholars who advocate the "interest-based approach" to negotiation argue that the parties' interests, whether stated or not, drive all negotiations, and one must therefore seek to know them to conduct or simply to understand any negotiation. The interests of individuals approached to participate in building an institution may vary widely from an ardent desire to further the institution's purpose, on the one hand, to a secret wish to sabotage the institution-building effort on the other.

An institution builder should use the recruitment process to learn about a group's or community's receptivity to embracing the proposed institution. As part of the launching process, the members of the working group at the outset should also agree upon the rules and procedures governing its activities and make them known to possible recruits.

A major problem in recruiting people to serve on the institution-building team is to identify the individuals to recruit. Institution builders, like sports team managers, usually know the type of person they want to recruit for the team, but they don't often know where exactly to find them. I faced this same problem when I became the chairman of the board of directors of two mutual funds, one specializing in Southeast Asian stocks and the other in Indian stocks. I had been a member of the boards of both funds for several years before becoming their chairman. Since neither fund had ever had a woman as a board member, I was determined to correct that deficiency the next time the two funds had an opening for a director. Within a year, that opening occurred as the result of a director's resignation. My colleagues on the boards agreed that we should concentrate our search for a replacement by finding a woman, but the more I thought about the matter, the more I realized that I did not know any woman who combined a knowledge of investment and finance with a substantive familiarity of the countries that were the focus of our two mutual funds. I therefore turned for help to one of the other directors, the late Lesley Gelb, a former president of the Council on Foreign Relations, *New York Times* editor, and senior government official, a man with impressively large network of acquaintances. I asked Les if he could recommend three women, preferably under 50 years of age with the qualities needed to serve as a fund director, whom we might interview for the job. Within a week, he sent me the names and short biographies of three excellent candidates. The other directors and I immediately interviewed them and were so impressed with two candidates that we decided to create an additional place on the board and hire two of them, an Indian-American with an MBA from Harvard and a Chinese-American with a master's degree from Yale. Both became valued members of the two boards. The moral of this story: If you don't know people who meet your recruitment needs, find someone who does know them.

3. Preliminary Agenda and Preparatory Measures

The institution-building team will need a preliminary agenda or at least a stated goal to guide its work at the outset. Without an agenda, the early discussions of the team are liable to consist of unfocused meandering talk that will waste time and, worse, demoralize its members. As important as an agenda is the designation of a team member to serve as chair to preside over the team's discussions and generally guide its activities. There are at least three options for designating a chair: (1) the person calling the meeting names a chair or a temporary chair in the invitation to the first meeting, having secured that individual's agreement to accept that role; (2) the meeting invitation names a temporary chair and states in the agenda that the first order of business will be the election of the institution-building chair; and (3) the invitation to the first meeting makes no mention of a meeting chair but implicitly leaves to the discretion of the team members the decision on whether, how, and when to designate a chair. That was precisely the process that led to my appointment as chair of Tufts Faculty Governance Group, an event that did not take place until its third week of meetings.

4. The First Meeting of the Institution-Building Team

The institution-building team's first meeting should be prepared with care. An important initial decision is determining the meeting site. The place you select can affect the process of the meeting and ultimately its result and may send both positive and negative messages to the participants.

For example, the first meeting of the Tufts Working Group did not take place on the premises of any of its eight schools but in a dining facility belonging to the central administration. It was a clear signal that the participants were engaged in a university activity rather than a school exercise. While video teleconferencing may avoid decisions on a particular site, they also limit human interactions necessary for building a team.

The preparations for what will take place at the launch meeting can also influence the success or failure of the team. Since that meeting may be the first time the team members have had any contact with one another, the organizers should make strong efforts to facilitate and develop cordial working relations among potential team members. As Chief Justice John Marshall understood, a catered meal or drinks reception can be an important first step in building constructive relations among team members. The lunch in a private dining room hosted by the Tufts president at the Faculty Governance Working Group's first meeting not only allowed the members to get to know one another in a relaxed environment but was also a clear signal that the university president and his administration considered the working group to be an important endeavor. At the same time, the organizers should be alert to the possibility that certain team members may have had unhappy or difficult dealings with other members in the past and that such troubled history may affect their relationship as members of the institution-building team.

The formalities of meetings may be important for a successful launch of an institution-building effort. Formalities of diplomacy are ways of acknowledging another country's status as a sovereign and equal member of the international community. Appropriate use of formalities, such as name tags, name plates, and brief biographies, can have the same effect in important business and social dealings. For example, in the negotiation of an alliance between Northwest Airlines and KLM, the Dutch air carrier, Northwest knew that KLM—a much smaller airline—was very sensitive about its status as an equal in the negotiations and later in the alliance. To alleviate these fears, Northwest structured all aspects from the shape of the negotiating table to the organization of social events as a meeting between two equal sovereign states. As one Northwest executive told me, "We used every symbol we could think of to recognize their individual sovereignties."

The organizers of the first meeting of the institution-building team might also seek to give the event a certain ceremonial tone to gain publicity for the endeavor, to affirm the importance given to the team's work, and to thank the team members for their willingness to devote their time and talents to helping to build a potentially important institution. To affirm these goals, the organizers of the meeting might invite a well-known official or other authority to give a short speech affirming the importance of the work of the institution-building team, thanking them for their service, and wishing its members success in their important endeavor.

As its work progresses and its understanding of its mission deepens, the institution-building team may decide to modify its objectives and amend its agenda to achieve its fundamental purposes. For example, the team working on selling the unprofitable corporate division may come to realize that no appropriate buyer exists and that a piecemeal liquidation of the division's individual assets is a better solution for the company.

Tools for Launching Institution Building

To launch the process of building an institution, potential institution builders need to bear in mind the following simple rules:

1. Prepare a clear statement of the institution to be built.
2. Identify and recruit the right people to work with you on building the institution.
3. Seek help in recruitment from knowledgeable people both within and outside the group committed to working on the new institution.
4. Reach an agreement with your team on the details of a first meeting to launch the project.
5. Select the right site for the meeting and prepare it carefully to serve the people attending the meeting.

CHAPTER 6

Task #2: Negotiating an Institutional Vision

The Role of Visions in Institution Building

Every builder needs a vision to make a structure. That vision may be found in elaborately detailed blueprints or roughly drawn pencil sketches. In either case, its purpose is the same: to guide the construction process to a desired end.

Institution builders also need a vision to arrive at their goals: functioning institutions that achieve desired social results. That vision is not usually found in a drawing on paper, but rather resides in the minds of institution builders. Its lack of physicality presents a special problem in carrying out the fundamental challenge of effectively conveying that vision to other institution builders engaged in constructing the desired institution. Words like "faculty senate," "shelter for battered women," "charter school," or other labels used to designate the goal of an institution each have many meanings and countless differing details that require painstaking specification and clarification if the ultimate result is to achieve its intended purpose. In and of themselves, these words are of limited use in building an institution.

Once a leader has formed an institution-building team, an important next task is therefore to negotiate a common vision of the proposed institution among its team members so that the work of institution building can proceed. Thus, the purpose of a vision is not only to guide the institution's construction, but also to serve as an agreement among its members as to how the institution will look and operate. Yet, a third function of a vision is to communicate the nature of a new institution to the outside world, particularly when broad social support for the institution is important. When Goldman Sachs, after 12 years of internal debate, transformed itself from a clubby closed partnership into a publicly traded corporation, that action clearly communicated to the world a vision that Goldman intended to become a global player in international finance and to gain a worldwide clientele. For all these reasons, it is important that the vision for the institution not reside in the institution builders' minds alone but that it be also reduced to writings, drawings, and other media so that it can be readily communicated to other persons.

Regardless of its purpose, creating a vision and rendering it into a format that can readily be understood is always a fundamental part of the institution-building process. The aim of this chapter is to provide guidance on creating institutional visions.

Looking for Vision

An initial question that institutional promoters may ask is: What is the source of institutional vision? Where do I find it? The almost reflexive response to that question by U.S. business writers and executives, influenced by American cultural values of individualism, is: "The organization's leader gives the organization its vision," pointing to examples such as Steve Jobs at Apple and Bill Gates at Microsoft. While leaders may play an important role in shaping and defining a vision for their organizations, they are usually not alone in the process of vision making, which is very often a collective effort. Indeed, many organizations' visions have been shaped by negotiations among its members.

Precedent is a powerful influence on human behavior. When faced with the challenge of creating something new, most people instinctively look for examples of how other people have done the same thing in the past. In short, they often look to models for help as a first step in institution building. The Tufts University Group on Faculty Governance did precisely that when it surveyed how other comparable universities had established their faculty senates before the Tufts working group started to make one of its own. It did its research by speaking with faculty members and administrators at those universities on their experience with faculty governance and by carefully examining the governing documents at other institutions because the Tufts group knew that the experience of other universities would provide valuable lessons for Tufts in establishing its own faculty senate.

In many years of working on law reform projects outside the United States, I constantly saw that government officials responsible for legal change in their countries were always eager to see and understand relevant legal models from other countries. The purpose of their search for models was twofold: education and legitimation. First, they believed that knowledge of foreign institutions would enable them to build more effective national institutions, particularly by helping them to shape more compelling visions of the institutions they were seeking to build. Second, their ability to show that a proposed institution had its origins or was like successful comparable institutions in other countries, particularly in developed countries, would influence acceptance of their proposal at home. Thus, a claim made to me many years ago by a banker in Sudan as he patted the top of his dusty metal desk that his bank was "still just like Barclay's Bank" was uttered with the hope of increasing its legitimacy in my eyes several years after the Sudanese government had nationalized it from Barclays.

Shaping a Vision

Based on the views of its leaders, the research it has undertaken, and the discussions among its members, the institution-building team will next seek to craft and express a vision for its work. To focus that effort, the team leader might engage the institution-building team in an exercise. Depending on the size of the group, the leader might divide the team into groups of five to seven people and ask each group during the following 30 minutes in separate meetings to discuss, agree upon, and prioritize not more than five of the most important qualities that the intended institution should have. After this period of separate consultation, the entire team should be convened in a general meeting to hear each group present and defend its choice of institutional qualities. Once each group has made its presentation, the entire team, under the guidance of a discussion leader, would seek to critique the choice of each group and, using a white board, seek to shape a consensus view on desired qualities of the proposed institution. Hopefully, this exercise may yield raw material for a formal vision statement.

The Vision Statement

Having studied useful models of a desired institution, the team should then move on to preparing a statement of its own vision of the institution that they contemplate making to serve their community or environment. No more than a single double-spaced page in length, the vision statement should set out succinctly the nature and purpose of the proposed institution. To start the process, the institutional promoter or a volunteer might prepare a one-page draft of a vision statement and then submit it to a critiquing and brainstorming team meeting of no more than two hours to prepare "a working version" that gains general acceptance from the team as forming a satisfactory basis for preparing an internal development plan for the institution and for discussing it with potential supporters.

Looking for Authenticity

A vision for an institution needs to be rooted in the culture and environment of the community it is intended to serve. In short, it must be authentic, if it is to gain and hold the support of that community. While it may have been inspired by a successful foreign model, it will fail like a delicate flower transplanted to a desert if it somehow cannot take root in the environment it is intended to serve. The importance of authenticity in institution building is illustrated by the law reform efforts that took place in northern Nigeria.

A Tale of Two Visions

In 1960, as Nigeria approached the agreed-upon date of its independence from Great Britain, the country's Northern Region, its largest and most heavily Islamic area, enacted the Northern Region Penal Code to replace the uncodified Islamic criminal law, found largely in the writings of Islamic scholars, that had been the basis for its criminal law since before the colonial era. The reason for the new code was the need to subject all persons in the Northern Region, regardless of religion, to a common body of criminal legislation, a condition seen as necessary for a newly independent country having an ethnically and religiously diverse population. To help write the new code, the Northern Region government created a commission of experts, both foreign and Nigerian, to advise it in drafting a new law by studying the experiences of other Islamic countries that had enacted modern penal codes while remaining faithful to Islamic legal traditions.

At the time, Northern Nigeria had two types of courts, state courts, conducted by the region's small number of legally trained judges and lawyers, which handled the most important cases, and the far more numerous "native courts," usually presided over by village elders, traditional Islamic judges known as *alkalis* and other persons with limited legal education, that handled approximately 90 percent of the judicial system's civil and criminal cases. Recognizing that the successful implementation of the new Penal Code and its related Criminal Procedure Code would clearly require a massive training program for the native courts judges and court administrators, the Northern Region Ministry of Justice asked the Institute of Administration, which had general responsibility for in-service training of the region's civil service, located on the Zaria Campus of Ahmadu Bello University (ABU) in the center of the Northern Region, to undertake the judicial training effort necessitated by the new laws.

That campus was also the site of the Northern Region's first and then only university law faculty, established in 1962. In September 1963, the U.S. Peace Corps African Lawyers Project had assigned me to assist in the development of the ABU Faculty of Law, whose first class of students was about to enter its second of a three-year LLB program, the university law degree required for the practice of law. In addition to teaching in that program, I became heavily involved in the training programs for native courts personnel and eventually developed and directed a diploma program in cooperation with the University of London for younger judges with significant secondary school education.

After two years of intensive work on those tasks, I left Nigeria in July 1965, with a strong sense of accomplishment, having assisted in graduating the ABU's first law faculty class, having developed a successful diploma program for judges, and having played a minor role, I thought, in the modernization of Nigeria's legal system. From the vantage of my plane heading north across the Sahara Desert, the future for Nigeria, Africa's most populous country, seemed promising.

In January 1966, a failed military coup assassinated Northern Nigeria's leadership, including Ahmadu Bello, the region's premier and a dominant political force in the country, an action that eventually led to a civil war that would last nearly three years. Afterwards, a series of military governments would rule the country (except for one brief period) for nearly 30 years until 1999 when democratic government returned to the country which by then had been divided into 36 states and a federal territory within the Nigerian Federation. With electoral politics returning to the country, one of the most salient political issues in many northern states was a demand to reinstall the Islamic law of crimes that the Northern Region Penal Code had abolished in 1960. Strong popular sentiment held that the 1960 Penal Code was "unislamic" (something that I had never heard anyone say during my entire time in Nigeria from 1963 to 1965) and that the rise in criminality perceived by the public was directly caused by the loss of Islamic law and its severe corporal punishments like flogging and stoning. For its opponents, the code was not an authentic institution but a foreign institution that violated their cultural and religious values and therefore should be drastically amended or repealed completely. Eventually, the legislative assemblies in 11 of Nigeria's states, exclusively in the northern parts of the region, with strong public support but over the opposition of their state governments, successfully adopted legislation to reintroduce Islamic criminal law.

The story of the 1960 Northern Region Penal Code and the re-islamization of the criminal law in parts of that former region 40 years later is actually a story about two visions of institution building. The governing elite in 1960 had a vision of the new Penal Code as an important step toward independence from Great Britain and the modernization of the country. Popular sentiment came to view the code as unislamic and a violation of their religion and culture. While certain elements of the population opposed the loss of the Islamic law of crimes, those in power in the early years of the penal law reform, and particularly the powerful Ahmadu Bello, believed they could placate any opposition to the new Penal Code and, moreover, saw it as merely a change in form rather than a change in substance. In any event, at the time of its adoption, the code encountered little, if any, popular opposition. It does not appear that the government in 1960 made any serious efforts at educating the public about the new Penal Code. Indeed, the government seems not to have considered the possibility of serious opposition to the proposed code at the time. After 40 years, with most of the code's advocates having left the

scene, its repeal became a winning issue in the election of a new genera-
tion of northern politicians.

Conclusions: Tools for Shaping Visions

In shaping a vision for an intended new institution, institution builders
should consider the following principles:

1. Institution builders should recognize that a vision statement of a
   proposed institution has three important functions: (1) to serve as
   a guide in building the institution; (2) to manifest an agreement
   among its builders about how the institution should function; and
   (3) to signal to the outside world that a new institution is about
   to emerge on the scene. The formulation of a compelling vision,
   expressed verbally or graphically, is therefore an important first move
   toward institutionalization.

2. To be most effective for these purposes, the vision guiding the creation of a new institution, while influenced by models of similar
   institutions, should take account of the culture and values of the
   people the institution will serve. Preceding the actual drafting of
   a vision statement, the members of the institution-building team
   might engage in an exercise to identify, express, and prioritize the
   most important qualities required of the proposed institution.

3. The promoters of the new institution should attempt to view
   the proposed institutions through the eyes of potential opponents
   and take steps to counter that opposition through education and
   negotiation.

4. No institution, no matter how long lived, is permanent. Because
   institutions are embedded in human societies, they are susceptible to
   the forces within those societies. Astute institution builders are aware
   of the ultimate fragility of their creations and seek to protect them
   from those forces as best as they can.

5. One important means of giving durability to a new institution in
   traditional societies is to adhere as closely as possible to local cultural forms in developing, introducing, and publicizing the new
   institution. To accomplish this task, seek advice from knowledgeable
   members of the culture in which you are working.

CHAPTER 7

Task #3: Negotiating an Institutional Plan

From Vision to Plan

To move from an institutional vision to an actual institution, institution builders need a strategic plan. A plan is a systematic sequence of actions to be taken to achieve a desired end. In athletics, a plan is a sequence of plays that will lead to a favorable score. In the game of institution building, the goal is a desired change in human behavior. The complexity, time, and cost of the plan will ordinarily depend on the nature of the institution to be built. An institution-building plan is not ordained by some high authority. The plan is usually a product of negotiations among institution builders and between institution builders and various stakeholders. Making an operational plan is the third vital task in building an institution. To be effective in virtually all cases, that plan must be reduced to writing, often in one or more detailed and lengthy contracts.

While the institution builders' vision will usually have set goals for their plan, the execution of that plan requires constant negotiation to take account of changing circumstances and unexpected demands along the way. Two factors, in particular, influence the negotiation of the institutional plan: (1) the nature and interests of the parties and (2) the nature of the institution they are trying to build.

To illustrate the complexities of negotiating plans for building an institution, this chapter will examine two cases: (1) the creation of the International Centre for Settlement of Investment Disputes (ICSID), an international institution built by states to provide dispute resolution services in conflicts between foreign investors and the countries in which they have invested, and (2) the creation of *Aguas Argentinas*, the world's largest water and sewage privatization at the time and an example of the thousands of privatized institutions created throughout the world over the last 30 years. Although each case is special, they both illustrate certain common principles of institution planning. A final section in the chapter will consider the lessons that each case teaches about the task of negotiating institutional plans.

Building a New International Institution: The International Centre for Settlement of Investment Disputes (ICSID)

One of the basic purposes of the World Bank as stated in Article 1 of its Articles of Agreement is "...to assist in the reconstruction and development of territories of members by facilitating the investment of capital for productive purposes...." In the early 1960s, the staff of the bank, led by the bank's General Counsel, Aron Broches, identified the risks of investment disputes between foreign investors and the governments of countries in which they invested and the lack of fair and effective mechanisms for resolving such disputes as factors inhibiting the international flow of investment capital. Noting that in earlier years the World Bank president had been asked on an ad hoc basis to help resolve specific international financial disputes, some of which involved foreign investors, the bank's General Counsel and his staff began to envision the creation of an international institution to settle such disputes.

Whereas private institutions such as the International Chamber of Commerce based in Paris, the London Court of Arbitration, and the Stockholm Chamber of Commerce were important providers of international arbitration services in conflicts arising out of international business transactions, they were private institutions based in capital-exporting countries, factors that led some developing country governments to question their impartiality in resolving disputes between foreign investors and the governments of countries in which they invested, particularly if they were developing countries. As a solution to this problem, Broches and his staff envisioned a new type of investment dispute resolution institution whose membership would consist of both capital-importing and capital-exporting states, instead of private corporations and entities. They felt that this mixed membership should give confidence in the fairness and independence of the proposed new institution's arbitration processes to both corporate investors from capital-exporting states who would become claimants and governments of capital-importing states likely to be respondents in foreign investment disputes. Moreover, unlike the private institutions mentioned earlier, the bank's legal staff envisioned the creation of an international institution founded upon a treaty among states.

The development of a consensus supporting the new institution within an international bureaucracy like the World Bank whose members were individual governments would be a complicated and lengthy process. In August 1961, Aron Broches would set that process in motion by sending a memorandum to the World Bank's Executive Board, an organ responsible for the bank's day-to-day operations, proposing the idea of creating such an institution under the bank's auspices. It was in effect the first step in an increasingly complicated negotiation.

Shortly afterwards, the bank's president, Eugene Black, endorsed the idea in his annual address to the bank's Board of Governors, the bank's principal organ of governance, and later in a memorandum to the bank's Executive Board, the group having responsibility for overseeing the bank's day-to-day operations. These preliminaries stimulated an internal dialogue on the idea, which culminated in a working paper by the General Counsel that included a draft "Convention for Resolution of Disputes Between States and Nationals of Other States," a document that would be necessary to establish an independent international institution governed by international law and engaged in investment dispute settlement as envisioned by the bank staff. The World Bank president asked the Executive Board to seek the views of their governments on the working paper. The draft convention was not only a proposed agreement by states to establish an international institution to provide dispute resolution services but also an operating plan specifying how such an institution would function.

The institution-building process then moved to a new, intermediate phase that focused on the details of the proposed institution and extended the dialogue to the governments of World Bank member states and to international experts outside the bank. Following a resolution of the bank's Board of Governors requesting the executive directors to study the proposal in depth, the executive directors, from December 1962 to

June 1963, meeting as a special "Committee of the Whole on Settlement of Investment Disputes," studied the working paper and the draft convention in depth. These discussions concentrated, on the one hand, on the general desirability of the dispute resolution proposal and, on the other, on the extent to which the World Bank should be involved in any resulting institutional arrangements. To obtain the views of legal experts from throughout the world, between December 1963 and May 1964, the bank held four Consultative Meetings of Legal Experts at the regional headquarters of the United Nations in Addis Ababa, Ethiopia; Santiago, Chile; Geneva, Switzerland; and Bangkok, Thailand. Immediately afterward, the staff of the bank issued another working paper consisting of a new draft convention based on previous discussions and meetings.

The bank's institution-building efforts moved into its final stages when it convened the Legal Committee on Settlement of Investment Disputes in Washington, which met 22 times from November 23 until December 11, 1964, with the participation of representatives of 61 governments. The committee undertook an article-by-article consideration of the draft convention. From time to time, whenever significant substantive disagreements were discovered, working groups (seven in all) were appointed, whose reports on specific questions were considered by the committee at a later stage. In addition, a drafting subcommittee considered each portion of the text of the proposed multilateral convention as soon as the committee reached a consensus on the item. The work of the Legal Committee culminated in the publication, on December 11, of the Revised Draft of the Convention. The principal changes between that draft and the previous first draft were summarized by the chairman in a report to the executive directors.

In January 1965, the bank's General Counsel submitted to the executive directors proposals for several minor drafting changes and the draft of a report which the executive directors could send to governments considering the adoption of the proposed convention. The executive directors, again meeting as a committee of the whole, first considered the draft convention at a series of seven meetings between February 16 and March 4 and made a number of changes; the committee then addressed itself to the draft report. Finally, on March 18, 1965, the executive directors formally adopted a resolution approving the text of the convention and their report on it, instructing the bank's president to transmit these documents to all the bank's member governments, and providing that a copy of the convention be signed on behalf of the bank to indicate its agreement to fulfill the various functions (principally those of the depositary) with which it was charged in the convention. Consequently, the bank's president on March 23, 1966, dispatched copies of the convention and the accompanying report to the governors and alternate governors of all World Bank members for their approval.

Following a procedure adopted in many multilateral treaties stating how they are to become effective, the Convention on the Settlement of Investment Disputes between States and Nationals of Other States specified that it would become effective 30 days after it was ratified by 20 states, an event which took place on October 14, 1966. The International Centre for Settlement of Investment Disputes, the institution created by that convention which was familiarly known as "the ICSID Convention," was founded on the same date. Over the years, many other countries would ratify the convention so that by 2023, ICSID had 158 member states, representing a broad array of the world's economic systems. Although ICSID did not register its first arbitration case until 1972, by 2022, it had registered 888 cases brought against governments from throughout the world with claims often rising to hundreds of millions of dollars and, in some cases, billions of dollars.

To resolve a dispute brought by an investor whose nationality differs from the country where the investment was made, the convention authorizes ICSID to establish, with the disputing parties' agreement, a separate independent arbitration tribunal, usually composed of three persons, appointed by the parties to the dispute, to hear and decide the dispute according to applicable legal rules and treaty provisions. Normally, the claimant and the respondent in a case separately appoint a member of the arbitral tribunal and the two sides then agree on a third person who is to serve as the tribunal president. If the two sides are unable to agree, the responsibility for appointing the third member falls on the president of the World Bank.

One may view ICSID as an institution incubator. Each arbitration tribunal created under ICSID auspices is a separate and independent institution. It is established for a particular case and dissolves when the case is terminated. Depending on the complexity of the case, the proceedings might continue for several years. I was president of an ICSID tribunal that functioned for 12 years.

With the World Bank serving as an institutional promoter, the negotiation of ICSID's institutional plan lasted approximately five years. The negotiation was complicated by the fact that the governments of all World Bank states were potentially participants in that process and had to be given the necessary deference due governments of a sovereign state. The second complicating factor was that the subject matter of the institution being promoted and negotiated was foreign investment, a highly political issue with varying governments having diverse positions and interests. In fact, at the same time that the World Bank was advancing the idea of creating an international institution to settle foreign investors' claims against host country governments, developing country governments formed a coalition to advocate at the United Nations General Assembly and elsewhere for the creation of a "New International Economic Order (NIEO)" that would give those countries enhanced economic opportunities and would, among other things, reduce the rights and privileges of foreign investors. Somehow, the two negotiations never became intertwined.

Viewed from outside, the processes of making the ICSID Convention and of establishing ICSID as an international institution appear heavily reliant on the seemingly interminable exchange of documents among governments and officials, diplomacy at its most boring; however, each of those exchanges was an important move in a negotiation among states that eventually led to an international consensus that gave a solid basis to the convention, a basis that has lasted almost 60 years and continues to attract new state members every year.

While the ICSID Convention is legally a multilateral treaty among states, it can also be viewed as the institution's strategic plan, resulting from over five years of negotiation, commencing with internal World Bank staff discussions and then spreading to interactions among governments of World Bank members. A document of 27 pages in its published form and 75 treaty articles long, the convention sets down the basic principles for the institution's establishment, financing, and governance, as well as the dispute resolution services of conciliation and arbitration to be offered by the ICSID.

Rebuilding the Old: The Negotiation of *Aguas Argentinas S.A.*

Many institution builders devote their efforts to rebuilding, renovating, or remodeling existing institutions, rather than constructing brand new ones. Since the late 1980s, governments have carried out a special kind of institutional renewal throughout the world under the banner of "privatization." Privatization is a process by which governments transfer state assets or state functions from the public or governmental sector to the private sector—in many cases to foreign private investors.

Beginning in the 1980s, both developed and developing country governments in many parts of the world engaged in vast efforts at privatization, so that by the year 2000, over a trillion dollars in assets in over 100 countries had been "privatized," that is, transferred from governmental to private hands.[1] Governments often undertook such actions with the encouragement and financial support of multilateral financial institutions like the World Bank and regional development banks like the Inter-American Development Bank. Depending on the country concerned, governments engaged in privatization with various goals including: (1) the reduction of governmental budget deficits caused by the annual need to subsidize inefficient public services, (2) the relief of debts incurred by state enterprises, and (3) the improvement in efficiency by placing government enterprises under private management that would hopefully bring them new capital, modern technology, equipment, and management skills. In most countries, the privatization of state assets requires an elaborate legal framework and, in many cases, some form of continued government regulation of the privatized enterprise. In all countries, the privatization of public services required widespread institutional change. Argentina was just one example.

During the 1980s, the Argentine economy and particularly the country's public service enterprises suffered from severe problems, including extremely high inflation, steep budgetary and fiscal deficits, a serious lack of investment capital, and no less than four monetary crises, each resulting in a currency devaluation of over 90 percent. Its state enterprises, particularly those providing public services, such as water, electricity, and sewage, suffered from underinvestment in their plants and services, poor management, overstaffing, and an inability to meet the demands and needs of the public. In metropolitan Buenos Aires, one result of this situation was a deterioration in the quality and quantity of water and sewage services provided to the public by the responsible state entity, the *Obras Sanitarias de la Nación* (OSN). From 1912 until 1980, OSN, a corporation owned by the federal government, provided water and sewage services throughout most of the territory of Argentina. In 1980, Argentina decentralized the water and sewage services, transferring their functions to provincial authorities, except for the City of Buenos Aires and certain surrounding municipalities, which remained the responsibility of OSN.

Buenos Aires, Argentina, is one of the world's great cities. A sophisticated city with a rich culture, it is the capital and commercial center of Argentina. In 1993, when the government undertook widespread privatization of its public services, the city itself had a population of slightly under two million people, but its metropolitan area, which includes the Province of Buenos Aires, had over 10.9 million inhabitants, 30 percent of whom had income below the poverty level.[2] Its state enterprises suffered the same failings as did those providing public services elsewhere in Argentina. As a result, metropolitan Buenos Aires experienced a serious deterioration in the quality and quantity of water and sewage services provided to the public by OSN.

In 1993, the area covered by OSN comprised the city of Buenos Aires and 17 suburban districts. Of the 8.6 million inhabitants in this area, only 5.7 million were connected to water supply and 4.9 million to sewerage. The lack of connections was concentrated in the poorer, suburban areas. The OSN system was also subject to sudden temporary stoppages. This resulted in a deterioration in the quality and quantity of water and sewage services provided to the public and the inability to expand the service to all inhabitants of the area, a situation that raised concern in the public and the press for the health and safety of the population.

In response to the deteriorating public services, the Argentine legislature enacted the State Reform Law in 1989, declaring the country's public services to be in a state of emergency and proposing a broad program of privatization to remedy the situation. The State Reform Law also invited the country's provinces to participate in the privatization process and authorized privatization of government entities in the fields of telecommunication, steel, transportation, and petrochemicals. The law offered the sketchy beginnings of a vision for significant institutional reform. Ultimately, that vision would lead Argentina to privatize approximately 90 percent of its state-owned companies between 1990 and 1994. Each privatization entailed the creation of new institutions to hold and manage the privatized services, as well as other institutions to regulate them. The privatization proceeds to the Argentine government ultimately exceeded U.S.$19 billion and were used largely to refinance and reduce public debt. The institutional promoters of Argentina's vast program of privatization were Carlos Menem, the country's president from 1989 to 1999, and Domingo Cavallo, Economy Minister and later Minister of Foreign Affairs.

In most countries, the privatization of state assets requires an elaborate legal framework and, in many cases, some form of continued government regulation of the privatized enterprise. The privatization of the Buenos Aires water and sewage system was no exception. It proceeded by a series of legal steps.

Having launched the process with the 1989 State Reform Law, the government of Argentina next enacted the Decree of October 5, 1990, to establish a framework for designating which public services, including OSN, would be privatized and transferred to private and foreign investors through a bidding process that would grant investors long-term concession agreements to run designated public services with an obligation to develop and modernize them.

In 1991, to control Argentina's inflation and depreciating currency that had inhibited both domestic and foreign investment, the Argentine government adopted the Convertibility Law which tied or "pegged" the value of the Argentine Peso to the U.S. Dollar—one dollar to one peso—and established a currency board, while requiring that the amount of Argentine currency not exceed the value of the country's foreign reserves.

Starting in 1990, the government added an international law dimension to its legal framework for investment, by concluding bilateral investment treaties, known as "BITs," to encourage international investment by firms in major capital-exporting countries. By 2000, Argentina had made 57 BITS, including one with the United Kingdom in 1990 and others with France and Spain in 1991. The purpose of the BITs was to promise investors from countries that had concluded BITs with Argentina that the government would grant them various levels of treatment, including no expropriation without compensation, the right to transfer profits out of the country, and fair and equitable treatment. In the event of a dispute between the Argentine government and the investors on whether the government's treatment met these treaty standards, Argentina agreed to submit to international arbitration to resolve the dispute. In 1991, Argentina also signed the ICSID Convention and, after its ratification, in 1994, became a member of ICSID on November 18 of the same year. All these actions were intended as a clear signal by the Argentine government to international investors that Argentina desired foreign capital and promised to treat it fairly.

On June 30, 1992, the Argentine government issued the "Water Decree"* to establish a regulatory framework for the privatization of OSN and to provide for the rights and obligations of the future concessionaire, the related regulatory bodies, and the users of the service. To attract the most qualified and experienced investors and to secure investment on the most favorable terms, the government also established a rigorous international bidding process with detailed bidding rules.

Based on the principles set down in the Water Decree, the Federal Ministry of Public Works and Services promulgated Bidding Rules (*Pliego de Bases y Condiciones*) that stated the object, terms, and rules of the concession; defined the bidding procedure; specified the rules concerning the concession contract; and set out a model of its desired concession contract. These rules, as subsequently revised, and the related model contract specified certain important provisions governing the financial aspects of the proposed concession, qualifications of investors, financial commitments, tariffs to be paid by consumers, and standards of efficiency to be achieved by the concessionaire. Argentina was not seeking just any investor, but an investor who would provide comprehensive and efficient service at lowest cost to users. The cost to users was determined by the government-approved tariff to be charged by the concessionaire to consumers for the service provided. Throughout the process, various international institutions,

---

* Decree No. 999/92, of 30 June 1992 (the "Water Decree").

particularly the World Bank and the Inter-American Development Bank, strongly supported Argentina's privatization program with advice, financing, and encouragement. The federal government actively publicized its desire to privatize public services and made significant efforts, including a road show in Brussels, to interest particularly qualified foreign enterprises to invest in the privatized entities, preparing and distributing a prospectus for this purpose. In addition, Argentina engaged the services of international consultants on both technical and financial matters related to its privatization efforts.

Attracted by what appeared to be a profitable opportunity, four experienced foreign water companies—Suez and Vivendi Universal (formerly Compagnie Générale des Eaux) from France, Sociedad General de Aguas de Barcelona S.A. (AGBAR) from Spain, and AWG Group Ltd. from the United Kingdom—formed a consortium with three local Argentine companies to bid on the concession. In December 1992, having been declared the winners of the bidding, the consortium began negotiations with the government on a detailed 30-year concession contract, covering the period 1993 to 2023. This complex document of 127 pages plus annexes specified the investors' rights and obligations, including investment commitments by the investors, rules for fixing the tariffs to be paid by consumers, and standards of efficiency to be achieved by the concessionaire. The concession contract and the related legal and regulatory frame together constituted the operating plan for Buenos Aires' new privatized institution for water and sewage.

The investor consortium also formed a new institution, an Argentine company, *Aguas Argentinas* S.A. (known as AASA), with an initial capitalization of U.S.$120 million, to hold and operate the concession. At the company's creation, AASA's capital stock was owned in the following proportions: (1) Suez (25.3 percent); (2) Vivendi (known at the time as Compagnie Générale des Eaux) (8 percent); (3) AWG (4.5 percent); and (4) AGBAR (12.6 percent). The four foreign investors thus held 50.4 percent of AASA's capital and had controlling interest in the new institution. The remaining capital came from local investors and AASA's Employee Stock Ownership Program (10 percent).

On April 28, 1993, AASA formally signed a 30-year Concession Contract with the Argentine government and, on May 1, assumed control and

management of the Buenos Aires' water distribution and wastewater systems, achieving the largest privatization of its type in the world. According to Argentine legal requirements, Suez was designated as the operator
of the concession with general management responsibility for the concession for which it was to receive 6 percent of AASA's gross revenues
from its services. Throughout its life, the concession remained subject to
strict governmental regulation and was an example of a "public–private
partnership" (PPP), a type of developmental institution favored by organizations like the World Bank.[†] The same consortium of foreign investors
would also win concessions to operate the water and sewage systems in
the Argentine Provinces of Santa Fe and Cordoba.

The concession contract required the investors not only to manage
the water and sewage systems but also to modernize and improve them
in very specific terms. By 2001, AASA had invested a total of U.S.$1.7
billion in the concession, an amount consisting of U.S.$120 million
in AASA's initial capital, U.S.$706.1 million in loans from multilateral
lending institutions (which the four foreign investors were required to
individually guarantee), and the remainder from cash flows generated by
AASA's operations. These investments led to substantial improvement and
expansion of the Buenos Aires' water distribution and sewage systems.
Between 1993 when AASA assumed the concession and 2005 when the
concession was near its end, the population with access to drinking water
increased from 5,559,270 persons to 7,859,000 persons (an increase of
41.37 percent) and the population with access to sewage services
increased from 4,532,856 persons to 5,989,000 persons (an increase of
32.12 percent). In addition, during that same period, the production of
drinking water grew from 3,398,000 cubic meters a day to 4,700,000
cubic meters a day (an increase of 33 percent); the sewage treatment
capacity increased from 27,305,000 cubic meters a day to 80,334,603
cubic meters a day (an increase of 194.20 percent); and the water network

---

[†] WORLD BANK, PUBLIC-PRIVATE PARTNERS] III'S REFERENCE.
Gu1131. VERSION 2.0 14. 2014. One definition of a PPP is: "A long-term
contract between a private party and a government entity, for providing a public
asset or service, in which the private party bears significant risk and management
responsibility, and remuneration is linked to performance."

expanded from 11,913 kilometers to 16,459 kilometers (an increase of 38.16 percent).[‡] Thus, it seems that the concession was achieving at least some of the goals that the Argentine government had sought in privatizing the Buenos Aires' water and sewage system.

During the eight-year period from 1993 to 2001, relations between the investors and the Argentine government appeared to be relatively harmonious and cooperative. Any difficulties encountered during that time were resolved amicably through consultations and negotiation. Since the concession was to extend over 30-years until the year 2023, the legal framework and the concession contract provided defined procedures for adjusting tariffs, investment commitments, and other factors, according to specified conditions, in the face of changing and unexpected circumstances. During the period between 1994 and 2001, the Argentine authorities agreed to two such major adjustments.

In the year 2000, however, this situation would change drastically as Argentina began to have significant difficulties in meeting its foreign financial obligations, eventually leading the country into the most serious financial crisis in its history, a crisis that would have grave consequences for its people and its investors, both foreign and national. It also began AASA's slow tango of death as the government took a series of measures that made it increasingly difficult to operate AASA at a profit. In 2001, the Argentine government ended the parity between the dollar and the peso, resulting in a 60 percent currency devaluation, and, at the same time, it refused to allow AASA to make adjustments in the tariffs charged to consumers according to the provisions of the concession contract. As a result, AASA ceased to operate at profit and to make payments on its multilateral loans, which led the lenders to demand that the four foreign investors individually make payments on the loan guarantees. Ultimately, in 2006, the government terminated the concession, alleging various faults committed by AASA. The water distribution and sewage systems were immediately transferred to a new public corporation owned,

---

[‡] Suez, Sociedad General de Aguas de Barcelona S.A., and Vivendi Universal S.A. v. The Argentine Republic, ICSID Case No. ARB/03/19 and AWG Group v. The Argentine Republic (UNCITRAL), Decision on Liability, 30 July 2010, para. 36, [hereinafter Aguas Liability Decision].

financed, and managed by the Argentine state, thus ending Argentina's 13-year experience with the privatization of the Buenos Aires' water and sewage system.

Since each of the four foreign investors was protected by a bilateral investment treaty made with Argentina by their home countries, they invoked their treaty rights and sued Argentina in ICSID arbitration for financial compensation for the losses caused by Argentina's actions. Their initial demands amounted to slightly more than U.S.$1 billion, with an additional claim for U.S.$20 million for attorney and litigation costs and a supplementary claim by Suez of U.S.$255 million for lost management fees. Ultimately, after several years of litigation, an ICSID tribunal determined in an award issued on April 9, 2015, that Argentina had violated the bilateral investment treaties protecting the four investors in that Argentina failed to treat them "fair and equitably" as the treaties required. The tribunal therefore awarded them slightly more than $400 million in damages. I served as tribunal president in the case.

The case did not end with the 2015 compensation award. Seeking to avoid payment of the award, Argentina proceeded to challenge the legal validity of the award in three different forums: (1) an ICSID annulment committee, an internal remedy allowed by the ICSID Convention; (2) the U.S. District Court for the District of Columbia, which had jurisdiction since the arbitration proceedings had taken place in Washington, DC; and (3) the U.S. Court of Appeals for the District of Columbia Circuit, which was asked to review the U.S. District Court's decision. All three forums rejected Argentina's challenges.[3]

Ultimately, in 2018, according to unofficial press reports, Argentina and the claimants negotiated a settlement payment of approximately $275 million, essentially a 25 percent discount from the amount awarded by the tribunal, thus closing the case after 15 years of an arduous, not to say costly, legal process.

It was also rumored that Argentina paid the investors not in U.S. dollars but in Argentine sovereign bonds.

Lessons of the Two Cases

The stories of ICSID and AASA appear very dissimilar at first glance. Upon further reflection, one sees that they have several strong similarities that reveal much about institution building. Essentially, they were both tales of institution building. The protagonists in each case were motivated by a vision that promised improvements in the status quo. In the case of ICSID, the visionaries were the bank's General Counsel, Aron Broches, and his legal staff, who envisioned a new type of international institution to resolve disputes between foreign investors and the countries in which they invested. The bank's staff also assumed that the existence of a dispute resolution institution in which investors have confidence would increase international investment. In the case of *Aguas Argentinas*, the visionaries were President Menem, Minister Domingo Cavallo, government officials, and the executives of foreign water companies who saw privatization of the country's water and sewage systems as a way to vastly improve the quality of those vital services and thereby better the lives of the country's population, while enabling the four foreign corporations to make a profit.

In both cases, the concerned institution builders had to carry out the tasks of institution building to successfully bring these two new important institutions into existence. They had launched and participated in two institution-building processes, negotiated bold visions of two new and imaginative institutions, developed elaborate plans for their birth, and successfully carried out those plans to make both institutions a reality. As the cases reveal, the institution builders in both cases devoted much time and effort to designing and negotiating detailed strategic plans to create the two central institutions, ICSID and *Aguas Argentinas S.A.* Moreover, the institution builders in each case were successful in that both institutions emerged from the building process as effective, successful organizations that delivered, at least at the outset, what its visionaries expected and promised.

And finally, throughout both cases, the important tool used by the institution builders in forging an institutional plan for ICSID and for *Aguas Argentinas* was negotiation. It was the means of transforming visions into realities.

Conclusion: Institution Builders' Planning Tools

1. Astute institution builders with a long-term perspective do not rely on oral agreements and general statements of goodwill by the parties as a basis for an institution. Instead, to establish an institution,

they insist on legally enforceable written contracts or treaties which meticulously define in detail the rights and obligations of the parties.

2. In most instances, an institution's plan is an agreement negotiated among institution builders and stakeholders and embodied in a written contract subject to law. The ICSID Convention, an international treaty governed by international law, was ICSID's institutional plan, and the *Aguas Argentinas*' institutional plan for the Buenos Aires' water and sewage concession was to be found in the various contracts between the investors, banks, and the Argentine government, along with the country's laws and regulations governing the privatized system.

3. The contract creating the institution will ordinarily provide for a specific dispute resolution to which the parties must refer in the event of a dispute. In many cases, one of the reasons for agreeing on special dispute resolution is to avoid the courts of one of the parties which may not be impartial or inefficient.

4. The parties usually intend institutional contracts to last many years or to be "permanent." The course of events sometimes frustrates these expectations. Astute institution builders often employ contractual or other devices to minimize the risks and costs of unexpected events. Investor–state arbitration and political risk insurance are two such devices.

5. The role of governmental regulators is key to the success of an institution, particularly one that serves the public. Their attitudes toward the institution will shift with changes in geopolitical forces. Understanding the intricacies of the prevailing regulatory system and building relations with regulators are essential to institutional survival.

CHAPTER 8

Task #4: Negotiating Institutional Resources

A resource is something or someone that helps or gives support to other people. All institutions need resources to come into existence and to function. To accomplish institutional goals, institution builders therefore need to know how to find and obtain resources. Indeed, it is impossible to conceive of the creation of an institution without resources. More than that, one may say a basic function of many, if not most, institutions, particularly those in corporate form discussed in Chapter 9, is to gather, hold, and invest resources to accomplish a valuable social purpose. The attributes of legal personality, limited liability, and ease of resource management offered by the corporate form in most societies are designed to encourage investment because those societies view investment as a social good. Without investment, the resources of society would lie fallow, and society would suffer a social cost. The fourth task that an institution builder must accomplish is to find and obtain the needed resources to build the desired institution. This chapter examines this vital task of institution building.

The Nature of Resources

One may divide resources into two general categories: physical resources and human resources. Physical resources are things, such as money, land, machines, tools, and supplies, that institution builders will need to create an institution. They are often referred to as physical "assets" and are accounted for on the left side of an enterprise accounting balance sheet. They may be acquired for the intended institution by sale, gift, lease, or loan, according to the terms of negotiated agreements between their owners and the individuals building the institution. Human resources, on the other hand, are people—people whose knowledge, skills, and labor are needed to build the institution and to enable it to function. Human resources participate in the institution-building process in all sorts of capacities—as partners, employees, consultants, advisors, experts, and volunteers. In international development, their contribution is known as "technical assistance." Their participation is secured by a negotiated agreement, formal or informal, written or oral, between them or their employers and the leaders of a particular institution-building enterprise. According to that agreement, they may engage in the process, with or without compensation, for a few hours, a week or two, months, several years, or even longer.

Resources and Institutional Leadership

The leaders of institution-building projects usually have the responsibility of securing the resources needed to build the desired institution. They gain that responsibility by virtue of their positions as leaders and the expectations of the people they lead. In the nonprofit world, securing resources for institution building is known as "fundraising" and in commercial ventures, it is often called "capitalizing" or "capitalization," or simply "raising capital." Functionally, despite the differences in labels and the subcultures in which they are pursued, fundraising and capitalizing play the same vital role in the process of institution building in both for-profit and not-for-profit endeavors. In both domains, no resources mean no institution.

During my career, I participated in several searches for university presidents and school deans. The ability of candidates to raise funds was always on the minds of the search committee members even though the word "fundraising" might have appeared nowhere in the job description. During the search for the SMU Law School deanship in which I was a candidate, a member of the search committee asked me, "Do you think you'll like fundraising?" "I'll like fundraising," I replied, "if I am successful at it." Although in retrospect my response seems a trifle flippant, my interrogator's message was very clear: "Fundraising is an important part of the job." Search committees are not the only ones evaluating a potential leader's fundraising prowess. Everyone who may work with that person on the institution-building project is silently asking the same question at their first meeting. "Will our leader be able to secure the funds we need to do this job?"

The Sources of Resources

To accomplish the task of obtaining resources, an institution builder must first identify the sources of that assistance. Resources for institution building may be obtained from within an institution to which an institution builder is attached or from outside that institution. For example, the resources to create the International Centre for Settlement of Investment Disputes (ICSID) came entirely from within the World Bank, while resources to establish *Aguas Argentina* were derived from sources both within and outside of the Argentine government. In either case, the acquisition of needed resources will require an institution builder to negotiate to obtain the resources from whoever is holding them.

The allocation of an existing institution's internal resources to the creation of a new institution is often the subject of debate within the institution requested to provide the resources. One issue of debate that arose during the foundation of ICSID was the extent to which the World Bank should be involved in ICSID's foundation and subsequent operations. Whether the future investment dispute resolution function should be placed in an independent institution or made a department of the World Bank was an important question that had implications for the bank's budget as well as the new institution's appearance of independence.

The guardians of an institution's finances often seem to resist instinctively efforts to allocate existing resources to new institutional endeavors since the guardians are the ones who will have to find ways to fill the budgetary hole created by the endeavor and will be blamed if the budgets that they manage end the year in deficit. In my second year as dean of the Fletcher School, Leila Fawaz, a faculty member who was a promising Middle East scholar holding a joint faculty appointment in the Tufts history department and the Fletcher School, informed me excitedly that the Middle East Studies Association had designated her the editor of its journal. I congratulated her, saying that the appointment would not only raise her profile in her profession but also boost the school's reputation.

She then said that she would need to establish an editorial office at the Fletcher and asked whether the school could provide her with funds to support her activities as editor, including the salary of an editorial assistant. She pointed out that when the journal was edited by a faculty member at another university, that person had received similar support. I told Leila that I was favorable to her request and would talk about it with Fletcher's associate dean for finance. When I raised the issue with the associate dean, he was resistant, arguing that the school had never provided funds for a journal published by another organization, that the faculty member had the obligation to raise her owns funds for her professional activities, and finally, "If you do this for her, you'll have to do it for everybody else on the faculty." I replied that the school had never had an opportunity like this before, that Leila was an excellent teacher and scholar deserving of our support, and that I was prepared to give similar support to "everybody else on the faculty" asked by a leading academic organization to edit its journal. He finally agreed to look for the funding in our budget and found it shortly after our conversation.

I never regretted my decision. Leila went on to become president of the Middle East Studies Association, to establish the Fares Center for Eastern Mediterranean Studies at the Fletcher School thanks to a substantial grant which she was instrumental in obtaining for the school, to serve as dean of Tufts University School of Arts and Sciences, and to write two highly regarded books on the Middle East. Institution building requires negotiation both within and outside of the institution builder's home institution. It's also important for institution builders to recognize that institution building includes building the knowledge and professional status of the persons working in the institution and that one of the many responsibilities of institutional leaders is not just to accomplish but to excel at that dimension of the job. In short, institutional leaders have the task not only of securing needed human resources but also of developing them. Institution building requires building the human resources already within the institution.

The specific array of available resources for institution building depends largely on whether the institution in question is for-profit or not-for profit. For-profit institutions generally rely on investments by investors, which may take the form of some mixture of equity and debt financing, as well as advice from consultants and advisors representing various specializations. *Aguas Argentinas S.A.*, the company that held the Buenos Aires water and sewage concession, discussed in Chapter 7, relied on financial and technical resources drawn from various quarters, including $120 million in equity provided by the four foreign corporations and $700 million in debt advanced by the International Finance Corporation, an affiliate of the World Bank, and the Inter-American Development Bank, owned by Latin American states for the purpose of contributing to the region's economic development. *Aguas Argentinas'* financial structure was an example of "project finance," often used in financing large infrastructure projects. In addition to its equity provided by its direct investors, project finance enterprises usually take on large amounts of debt from banks and other financial institutions on the assumption that the enterprise will repay the loans over time from the project's earnings. Since project finance loans have a certain amount of risk of nonrepayment, lenders often require guarantees of repayment from third parties involved in building the new institution, as was the case with the loans to Aguas *Argentinas* by the International Finance Corporation and the Inter-American Development Bank, which required each of the project's four wealthy foreign investors to guarantee the loans. In addition to the providers of financial resources to the project, various international consulting companies assigned human resources to advise the Argentine government on building its new privatized institution for providing water and sewage services to the province of Buenos Aires.

The array of resource providers available for institution builders is potentially broad, but the ability of a particular institution to attract resources from a given donor usually depends on a host of variables including the nature of the specific recipient and its leadership, the donor's institutional mission and the interests of its leadership, and whether the potential recipient is a nonprofit or for-profit institution. Generally, except for bank loans and philanthropic gifts, private capital play a less important role in providing resources for building nonprofit institutions than they do with for-profit institutions. Second, governments, international organizations, and private foundations are important sources of support for nonprofit institutions. For example, the staff of the World Bank, with support of the bank's member state governments, conceived and established the ICSID, discussed in Chapter 7, without any resources from the private sector. Once established, ICSID would be financed by annual allocations from the bank's budget and the proceeds from the fees paid by litigants to ICSID for the institution's dispute resolution services.

The World Bank and other international agencies provide both financial aid and technical assistance to institution-building efforts considered to have important developmental results. For example, the World Bank supported my work of helping Laos write a new company law and my participation in a team preparing a strategic plan to strengthen Indonesia's legal system.

Governments, particularly through their foreign relations and international development budgets, as well as foundations and consulting firms, are important sources of funds and technical assistance for institution building. My work helping to build a law faculty in Nigeria was sponsored and supported by the U.S. Peace Corps, my participation in Egypt's efforts to create new institutions in support of its "openness policy" was underwritten by the Ford Foundation, and my work training officials from ministries of finance and central banks as part of the Fletcher School's program on "financial inclusion" was funded by annual grants to the school from the Bill and Melinda Gates Foundation for nearly a decade. Each of these programmatic efforts was the product of careful study and negotiation by the donors and the recipients of the support provided to assist in institution building.

Some people think of foundations as a kind of Santa Claus, an entity with bags of money ready to be handed out just for the asking. In fact, most modern foundations have carefully determined through study the areas in which to invest their money and just as carefully evaluate the potential recipients and projects they will fund. They also regularly evaluate the effects of their philanthropy to determine whether their grants did in fact achieve the foundation's goals and whether they should continue their support. Consequently, institution builders seeking foundation support should devote significant time to reviewing foundation reports on their activities and in preparing proposals for funding. They should also seek to arrange meetings with the relevant foundation program officers so that both sides can get to know each other well. The purpose of these meetings is to build a relationship between the foundation and the potential recipients of its generosity. If the office visits proceed well, the foundation officers may ask to pay a site visit to a potential recipient's location. Through this relationship-building process, the foundation will gain confidence that the recipient will effectively spend grant funds to achieve both the foundation's and the institution's stated goals.

After the institution has received the grant funds, wise institution builders will work at maintaining and strengthening their relationships with the foundation's officials. A relationship implies a *connection* between the parties, a complex set of continuing interactions characterized by a degree of cooperation and hopefully trust. To maintain and strengthen existing relations, the following three rules may help: (1) communicate regularly with the program officers at the foundation, including your ideas for new projects; (2) invest time, including occasional visits to the foundation and invitations to the foundation program officers to visit the recipient institution; and (3) always seize on opportunities to express your and your institution's thanks for the foundation's help.

Institution builders should be aware that most foundations don't want to become a permanent source of support for a recipient institution. Some foundations have shorter attention spans than others. So, wise institution builders should have plans to make a transition to other sources of support when the foundation that has been supporting them says "goodbye."

The Tools for Resourcing Institutions

Institution builders' ability to secure resources for their institutions depends on a variety of talents and techniques, but two of their most important tools are antennas and networks. Just as certain members of the animal kingdom depend on the antenna attached to their bodies to gain valuable information about prey, institution builders depend upon their diverse connections and links to the outside world to learn about funding opportunities. After evaluating the opportunities, they rely on their networks to tap those resources for their institutions. An example is my own experience in landing a major gift from a large Japanese multinational corporation.

In early 1985, while I was dean of Southern Methodist University's School of Law in Dallas, Texas, I received in the mail an engraved invitation to attend a formal dinner in Washington, DC, celebrating the founding of the Hitachi Foundation in the United States by the Hitachi Corporation, one of Japan's largest conglomerates. The invitation noted that Delwin Roy, an economist with whom I had worked closely at the Ford Foundation on the Egyptian investment program, had been appointed president of the foundation. Reluctant at first to devote two whole days just to have dinner in Washington, I ultimately decided to attend out of respect for my friend Del Roy. The dinner was a glamorous affair, with members of the Washington elite in attendance. One notable at the dinner was Elliot Richardson, who had held four cabinet positions under Presidents Nixon and Ford and gained fame for resigning in protest as Attorney General when he refused Nixon's order to fire Archibald Cox, the special counsel investigating Nixon's role in the Watergate scandal. At the time of the dinner, Richardson, then in private law practice, was serving as chairman of the Hitachi Foundation's board of directors.

The dinner in Washington turned out to be a pleasant affair. It was clear that in creating the foundation, Hitachi was seeking to build its relation and reputation in the United States at a time when certain parts of the American public were hostile to Japan because of its perceived unfair trade practices. When I returned to Dallas, it was not yet clear where in the United States the Hitachi Foundation would devote its resources, but there was little doubt that a law school in Texas would not be a potential beneficiary, so I did not think much about the contacts I had made at the Washington dinner.

Within a year, that would change when I was appointed dean of the Fletcher School of Law and Diplomacy at Tufts University, the oldest graduate school of international relations in the United States. As the Fletcher faculty and I began to shape a strategic plan for school's curriculum, we identified the role of technology in international affairs as a topic that needed greater scope in our curriculum and more serious attention in our research. It then occurred to me that what the Fletcher School needed was a Center of Technology and International Affairs to explore the issues on a permanent basis and that the Hitachi Corporation had the money to pay for it, starting with a grant of a million dollars as endowment to put the center on solid footing. I raised the idea of a grant from the foundation to launch the Fletcher Center with Del Roy, the president of the Hitachi Foundation, but he said a million dollars for a single grant was way beyond the foundation's spending limits. He did say that the Hitachi Corporation might be interested in establishing a Center for Technology and International Affairs and that he would put me in contact with the right Hitachi executives to approach. The alumni office at the school also reminded me that Fletcher had a strong and influential alumni network in Japan with many leading diplomats and officials and that I should be sure to mobilize them behind the idea of creating a center of technology and international affairs center at the Fletcher School.

On my first visit to Japan as Fletcher dean, I met with Hitachi executives to discuss the technology and international affairs center and received a polite but not overwhelmingly positive response. On the other hand, the Fletcher alumni association in Tokyo was very enthusiastic.

Over the next two years, I visited Tokyo once every six months and, each time, met with Hitachi executives. Each time, their response was polite but noncommittal. The lack of enthusiasm was disheartening and made me think about dropping the idea of persuading Hitachi to give the school a million dollars. On the other hand, it seemed to me that, with each meeting, the seniority level of the executives in attendance grew higher. Finally, at the end of the second year, I had a very cordial meeting with the chairman of Hitachi, who accepted my invitation to visit the Fletcher School, so I became confident that a grant of funds was likely. Shortly after my return from Tokyo, I received a note from the Hitachi corporate secretary saying that the Hitachi board had approved our request and that we would be receiving the funds shortly. Since it had taken Hitachi over two years to consider and approve our request, I was not optimistic that we would receive the money any time soon. So, three days later, I was astonished to receive a call from the Tufts University Treasurer's Office, saying "We just received a million dollars from Tokyo, earmarked for Fletcher. What do you want us to do with the money?"

We almost immediately set up an endowment account for the benefit of the Hitachi Center of Technology and International Affairs. Shortly thereafter, the center came into existence and continues to function today as a dynamic institution of teaching and research.

The Search for New Resources

Robust institutions are always looking for new sources of resources. In 1991, Nathan Gantcher, then chairman of the Tufts University Board of Trustees and the president of Oppenheimer, an established Wall Street financial firm, called me and asked, "Do you know something about emerging market countries?" When I said that I did, he explained that Oppenheimer with Salomon Brothers, another highly regarded financial firm, was planning to launch a mutual fund that would offer U.S. investors the opportunity to invest in dollar-denominated government bonds issued by certain developing countries. He then asked whether I would be interested in serving on the board of the new fund. When I said that I would be interested, he said that one of his associates would shortly be in touch with me to work out the details.

The year 1991 was the height of the economic globalization movement and the "Washington Consensus," a set of free-market policies that encouraged developing countries to commit to free trade, privatization, and foreign investment. In response, certain advanced developing countries with strong foreign trade markets began to issue U.S. dollar-denominated government bonds, having decided that this financing method gave them more favorable terms for their borrowings than international bank loans, their only previous option for obtaining U.S. dollar credits. Once issued, these bonds were traded in the secondary market. Many of these bonds gave investors handsome returns.

The foreign sovereign bond market is no place for small or even medium investors. It requires large amounts of capital, specialized knowledge of a relatively closed market, and an understanding of the geopolitical forces that influence the pricing of sovereign obligations. For Gantcher and his associates, the means to bring this market to the average American retail investor lay with a specialized institution—the closed-end mutual fund. Their plan was to form a Maryland corporation for the purpose of investing in developing country sovereign bonds, sell its mutual shares in an initial public offering (IPO) according to U.S. laws and regulations to American investors, make a management contract with a firm specializing in investing and managing sovereign debt instruments, and then invest the proceeds of the IPO in foreign government bonds whose prospects were determined to be promising by the mutual fund's management team. The fund shares sold in the IPO would be listed on the New York Stock Exchange, allowing U.S. shareholders to exit and new investors to enter the fund at will.

Oppenheimer's first IPO, the Emerging Markets Income Fund, was favorably received in the market and proved to be a success. As a result, in the next few years, Oppenheimer and Salomon Brothers launched the Emerging Markets Income Fund II in 1993, raising over U.S.$320 million, followed by other closed-end funds offering investments in various types of developing country sovereign bonds. In 1993, after India had changed its policy in 1991 radically to open the country to foreign investment, Oppenheimer established the India Fund, a closed-end fund listed on the New York Stock Exchange with the purpose of investing in the shares of Indian companies, listed principally on the Mumbai Stock Exchange. Its IPO was also successful, yielding almost $1 billion. Each of these new mutual funds was an institution, and their institution builders were investment banks. I served as member of the funds' boards of directors and chairman of the board of the India Fund. The creative use of institution building allowed investment banks to introduce U.S. investors to financial markets that had, for practical reasons, previously been closed to them. The resulting introduction of U.S. investment in these foreign securities had the probable effect of strengthening the market for developing country securities and thereby reducing the developing country's cost of capital.

Conclusion: Institution Builder's Resource Plays

1. By virtue of their position, institution builders have the responsibility to find and secure the resources necessary to build the institution.
2. Institutional resources are both physical and human.
3. Securing the necessary resources is always a process of negotiation, even in cases of philanthropic and charitable gifts to the institution. As in hunting prey, a fruitful negotiation begins with a thorough understanding of potential donor's interests.
4. Once the gift is received, the negotiation continues as the institution builder lays the groundwork for subsequent gifts.
5. Like a sports team coach, institution builders should have a plan for developing the human resources that come to the institution.

CHAPTER 9

Task #5: Legalizing the Institution

To operate in any country and to benefit from the privileges offered by its government, an institution must comply with that country's laws. An important task for any institution builder, often aided by a qualified lawyer, is therefore to be sure that the institution meets the demands of the country's legal system and that mechanisms are in place to preserve its continuing legal status in the future.

For institution builders, the task of legalizing an institution has various purposes. Two of the most important are, first, to gain the new institution legal recognition as an entity separate and apart from the persons who are organizing it and, second, to entitle it to take advantage of various rights and privileges that the governing legal system grants to such institutions. The purpose of this chapter is to provide guidance to institution builders for carrying out both tasks.

In 1989, I was elected the first president of the Association of Professional Schools of International Affairs (APSIA), which, prior to that time, had been a loose network of international relations schools at nine universities. At that time, its only activity had been a one-day meeting of the schools' deans and administrators twice a year. As the organization's first president, my mission was to transform that network into a functioning institution.

An important first step was to establish APSIA as a nonprofit corporation so it would become a legal entity that existed and functioned separately from the individual member schools. An equally important second step was gain for APSIA the status from the U.S. Internal Revenue Service of a tax-exempt "501(c) (3) organization" so that the gifts and grants it received would not be taxable to APSIA and, at the same time, would be deductible from the donor's own taxes. We hoped that APSIA's status as

501(c) (3) organization would assist its fund-raising efforts. This legalization process also gave the organization a legal structure that allowed it to grow over the years from a loose association of 9 schools in 1989 to the point that by 2023 it had 40 university members and 26 affiliates from throughout the world.

Similarly, when I chaired the task force that created Tufts University Faculty Senate to give the faculty a voice in university governance, an important initial question was to decide on the institution's legal basis. The task force determined that the decision to create the proposed faculty senate should be authorized by and its bylaws incorporated into a formal decision of the university's Board of Trustees, the university's governing authority. The task force members felt that a decision by the trustees would give the senate permanence and protect it from any efforts by future presidents or other administrators who might by unilateral action seek to reduce the senate's powers. The lesson of these two stories is that institution builders should be alert to legal issues required by their job and ready to find legal help when the need arises.

The Advantages of Corporate Existence

An institution that gains the legal status of a corporation or a company (the specific terminology depends on the applicable national or state law) acquires certain important advantages. Most countries and American states have two different company or corporation laws: one for business entities and one for nonprofit institutions. Unlike business corporations, nonprofit corporations may not be formed for profit or financial gain, nor may their corporate assets, income, or profits be distributed to the corporation's members, directors, or officers unless permitted by law. The advantages of corporate existence are largely the same for nonprofit and for-profit institutions. Institution builders should particularly be aware of five advantages:

1. Companies and corporations are legal entities that are separate and distinct from the people who manage them or have financial interests in them. Thus, they are said to have "legal personality" and to be "legal persons." As a result, institutions that become companies

or corporations may hold, acquire, and transfer property in their own names, make contracts, sue and be sued in their individual capacities, and engage in legal transactions just as physical persons can. By forming a nonprofit corporation, APSIA transformed itself from a loose informal association of nine schools whose leaders met for dinner twice a year into a single legal entity that was separate from the nine schools that created it. The leader of a large U.S. philanthropic foundation strongly encouraged this effort when he told me and another dean that his foundation's principal interest was in strengthening international affairs education generally rather than supporting individual schools. He felt that, by forming a corporation, APSIA would undertake the kind of broad range, multi-school programs that his foundation would want to support.

2. As entities existing apart from their founders and managers, companies and corporations usually have an unlimited life under most legal systems. This factor gives stability to institutions in corporate form since their legal existence is unaffected by the entry and departure of individual managers, officials, and investors. Thus, since APSIA's foundation as a corporation in 1990, some 30 individuals have served as its president and over 30 universities have joined it as a member. None of these events affected APSIA's status as a corporation or its basic structure.

3. Shareholders in companies and corporations benefit from "limited liability," which means that they are not liable for the debts and obligations of companies in which they have invested. It was for this reason that the lenders to *Aguas Argentinas S.A.* (AASA), discussed in Chapter 7, required guarantees from its foreign investors to pay the loans that AASA received from multilateral lenders if AASA failed to do so. Similarly, employees and managers in nonprofit corporations are not personally liable to repay the debts and obligations of institutions that they work for, unless of course they too have made personal guarantees.

4. The corporate structure allows centralized control and management by a few managers of the assets and operations of a potentially diverse, vast, and widely dispersed enterprise. This structure facilitates the development of easily controlled groups of corporations,

often located in many different countries. In fact, one of the most discussed types of international investor, the "multinational corporation," is legally not a single corporation at all but rather many corporations and companies that are linked together by share ownership.

5. The domestic law of the country concerned usually allows shareholders in business corporations and members of nonprofit corporations to enter and exit their organizations without affecting the legal structure of the underlying entity.

In most U.S. states, the process of forming either a for-profit corporation or a nonprofit corporation is relatively easy and inexpensive. Because of its organizational advantages, the formation of corporations deserves a place in any institution builder's toolbox.

Negotiating With Governments

For their institutions to operate legally, institution builders must often obtain approvals or resources from one or more governmental agencies. For example, to establish a charter school, its founders may have to receive approval from a state's department of education and budgetary support from a local school district. To export advanced technology to a foreign country, a U.S. corporation will have to obtain an export license from the U.S. Department of Commerce. These approvals don't just drop in the laps of institution builders. In most cases, to get what they want from governments, institution builders will need to negotiate. Negotiation is an important tool for gaining the needed government approvals and resources.

An experienced international executive once told me that, compared to negotiating with private companies, negotiating with governments "feels different." The reason that governments feel different is that they enjoy special powers and are subject to special constraints that commercial companies do not have. Those special powers include having a monopoly position (e.g., your state's department of education is the only agency in the state that has the power to approve charter schools), enjoying special governmental privileges and immunities (e.g., government agencies are protected from civil suits in some situations), their position as recognized defenders of the public interest and welfare (e.g., they can justify all their actions as "done in the public interest"), and their ability to use special protocols and forms in conducting negotiations. At the same time, governments are subject to special constraints in their negotiations that private corporations do not have, including the legal rules that they must follow in conducting negotiations, pressures from their political constituents, bureaucratic incentives and interests of their organizations, and the operational norms that they must follow in dealing with the public.

The following short case study illustrates the challenges of negotiating to legalize a new institution.

A Case of Negotiating for a Tax Exemption in Sudan

In the mid-1970s, the Ford Foundation appointed me as its first representative in Sudan, a struggling developing country on the Nile just south of Egypt. To establish an office and begin development program activities in Sudan, I first had to negotiate a "country agreement" with the Sudanese government, allowing the foundation to operate in its territory. The Sudanese Ministry of Foreign Affairs was the government agency responsible for concluding such agreements, so I arranged a meeting at the ministry in Khartoum, the country's capital, to discuss the issue with a Sudanese diplomat responsible for relations with foreign aid organizations. The official with whom I was negotiating the country agreement was a bright and polished diplomat who had graduated from the University of Khartoum Law School with which the Ford Foundation had a long association. He was extremely cordial and seemed eager to encourage the foundation to expand its activities in the country.

After some pleasant preliminaries and a couple of cups of sweet tea, our discussions moved quickly to the various issues to be included in our country agreement. As I outlined what the foundation needed to establish an office and undertake programs in the country, he readily agreed to all I requested. However, as a final item, when I explained that we would also require a complete exemption from all taxes and customs duties both for the foundation and for its personnel, the agreeable smile on his face was replaced with a look of consternation. Tax and customs exemptions for a purely private organization? The foreign ministry had never done that before. The Sudanese diplomat wasn't sure whether the ministry even had the authority to grant such an exemption. Even if it did, he didn't know whether the government would be prepared to grant exemptions to a wealthy foreign organization like the Ford Foundation. Clearly, there were no definite rules on the topic, and that presented a problem to my counterpart and, by extension, to his superiors in the ministry. At that point in our negotiation, it looked as if Sudan was not going to grant a tax exemption to the Ford Foundation. If that happened, I was fairly sure the foundation would drop the whole idea of establishing an office in Sudan.

Like any other person negotiating with the government, I needed to find a way to influence a government official's decision in my favor as we struggled over the issue. I tried to explain to the Sudanese diplomat that what I was asking for was really not that unusual and that in all the countries in which the Ford Foundation had offices, the local government had granted it an exemption from taxes and customs duties. He nodded in understanding, but hardly seemed convinced. I then said that the foundation had such a country agreement for many years with Egypt, which was the regional center office for all its activities in the Middle East, including programs in Sudan. If the foundation didn't establish an office in Khartoum, it would be forced to operate its Sudanese programs from Cairo. Suddenly, the Sudanese diplomat brightened and said, "I would like to see the Egypt country agreement. Do you think you can get me a copy?" I said that I would try.

The next day, before being able to contact our Cairo office using Sudan's uncertain international communications system, I received a telephone call from the foundation's representative in Egypt. "What are you stirring up down there? Two guys from the Sudanese embassy here just showed up unannounced at the office and asked to see a copy of our country agreement with Egypt. Should I give it to them?" With my encouragement, he sent a copy of the foundation's Egypt country agreement to the Sudanese embassy in Cairo, which then forwarded it by diplomatic pouch to the foreign ministry in Khartoum. The following week, the Sudanese diplomat and I agreed on a complete text of a country agreement between the Ford Foundation and the government of Sudan. Its provisions on tax and customs exemptions followed the text of our Egyptian country agreement word for word.

This case illustrates the power of precedent in government negotiations. It demonstrates the importance of finding the right precedent when you prepare for your negotiation with a government. A first step in finding the right precedent is to put yourself in the position of the government officials with whom you are negotiating and to look at the issues under discussion from their point of view. Go through an analysis identifying the questions that are most probably in the minds of your counterparts and then think about the precedent or standard that will answer those questions. Remember every negotiated agreement is a prediction about the future, a prediction about benefits and costs. My goal in negotiating a tax exemption with Sudan was to convince the Sudanese that the exemption would yield the country maximum benefits at little cost. One way of assuring them that my prediction was justified was to show them what had happened in a similar case in Egypt.

You may have several precedents to choose from. In making your choice among possible options, you should be guided by two important criteria: specificity and relevance. The more specific you can be about the details of the precedent, the more persuasive you are likely to be in convincing government officials or regulators that the precedent ought to govern their actions in their negotiation with you. For example, my statement to the Sudanese diplomat that the Ford Foundation had tax exemption agreements with many countries was less effective than my reference to the specific case of Egypt. Specific cases and concrete facts have a way of seizing the attention of other people more effectively than do generalities. More importantly, the specific case seemed to afford greater assurance that the deal will happen as predicted than would a bland general principle.

Second, the specific case that you choose needs to be relevant to the issues under negotiation. For the Sudanese diplomat, the example of the Egyptian country agreement was probably the most persuasive relevant precedent I could have given because of Egypt's long and close relationship with Sudan and its similarity in culture and political outlook. To have cited the foundation's country agreement with Indonesia or Brazil although helpful would have been much less convincing. Finding a precedent that is exactly like the case you are negotiating is often difficult and sometimes impossible. In those situations, your task as a negotiator is to show how a past case that is apparently different from the one under negotiation is actually relevant.

Finding an appropriate precedent for your negotiation can be more difficult than locating the applicable law, regulation, or rule since laws, regulations, and rules are usually published in an accessible form. Precedents often are not. Appropriate precedents are sometimes stored only in dusty filing cabinets and in people's memories. Some may be reported in the press, but some are not. One means of uncovering these precedents is to talk to people in relevant government offices and in the communities affected by those offices.

"It's Never Over"

Institution builders need to bear in mind that one of the risks of negotiating with governments is their tendency to view any deal they make as open to reconsideration and renegotiation, even after the contract has been signed, when it suits government interests. Suppose that last year your state's department of education authorized you to establish and operate a K-12 charter school and that your local school board also agreed to let you use one of its buildings for classes free of charge. This year, the department of education is imposing new and costly teaching training requirements on your school, and the local school board is asking you to pay rent for the building you are using. You are now faced with renegotiating two deals that you thought were over and done with. Former Secretary of State George Shultz, an experienced government operator, captured the essence of this phenomenon when said about recurring political negotiations, "It's never over."[1] In effect, your negotiation with the state department of education and your local board of education were never really over, despite the fact that you have signed contracts with both agencies. Since the risk of renegotiations is ever present in dealing with governments, institution builders should incorporate into their negotiation strategies and mechanisms to deal with the risk. Here are a few suggestions for institution builders to consider:

1. Make efforts after signing contracts to preserve the relationships that you developed in negotiating them. The existence of a relationship

between the parties is likely to make the resolution of subsequent conflicts easier than if no relationship existed.

2. Resist the temptation to make moralistic or belligerent statements in response to demands for renegotiation of signed contract but seek instead to understand the basis of the demands.

3. Consider a role for a mediator or other third-party helper in the renegotiation.

4. Look for ways to advance your interests in the renegotiation. For example, the negotiation with the school board for rent might be the time to obtain a desired extension on the length of your lease.

Conclusion: Institution Builders' Tools for Negotiating With Governments

As institution builders prepare and conduct negotiations with governments, they should bear in mind the following principles:

1. Never challenge the authority of a government official or department. All government agencies jealously guard their authority because authority is what allows them to govern. Respect and deference should guide all your negotiations with any government. Bear in mind the wisdom of Admiral Hyman Rickover, the developer of the U.S. nuclear submarine and a tough bureaucratic infighter in his own right: "If you're going to sin, sin against God not the bureaucracy. God will forgive you, but the bureaucracy won't."

2. Learn the rules governing the negotiation process and the protocols and forms expected of you as a nongovernmental negotiator. To gain that knowledge, seek the advice of consultants, people living in the community concerned, and those individuals who have had experience in negotiating with the governmental unit with which you are dealing. In seeking to understand the professional and personal interests of government negotiators, always search for the political imperatives influencing their decisions. The political imperatives to which government negotiators respond are usually to defend themselves against political opponents; to retain the support of vital

constituents; and to preserve their resources, autonomy, authority, and career prospects.

3. Understand that government negotiators usually fall into one of three classes: politicians, political appointees, and bureaucrats. It's important to analyze how each group's particular interests and worldviews may affect the negotiation. Be sure you know in which category your counterpart on the other side of the table falls.

4. Before beginning the negotiations, institution builders should consult with officials informally about their plans and try to learn as much as possible about the way a particular department handled similar applications in the past.

5. Frame your proposals in ways that accord with government interests, official policies, and the political imperatives of your counterparts at the negotiating table.

6. Always look for a precedent to support your request or proposal. The most influential precedents are those that are specific and relevant to the issue you are negotiating and are well established by having been followed many times in the past. New approaches on the other hand often raise concern with insecure officials who fear that a departure from a precedent will open them to challenge and attack by their bureaucratic superiors and adversaries.

CHAPTER 10

Task #6: Promoting the Institution

All the tasks that we have considered thus far relate to the design and construction of institutions. Another important task that some but not all institution builders may be called upon to undertake is to promote the acceptance of the proposed institution by important elements or groups within the society, acceptance that is essential if that institution is to govern the social activities for which it was designed. To gain that necessary acceptance, institution builders will often undertake campaigns of persuasion. In devising those campaigns, institution builders need to ask three fundamental questions: (1) Who needs to be persuaded? (2) What messages will persuade them? (3) How should those messages be delivered? This chapter will seek to answer those questions.

The promotion of an institution generally has one of two basic purposes: (1) to secure the enactment of the necessary approvals of the proposed institution by a society's governmental authorities and (2) to encourage the members of that society to use the institution. The first type of promotion might be called "Institutional Enactment Promotion" and the second "Institutional Use Promotion." In most cases, institution builders will have to engage in both types of promotion. The targets and, therefore, the methods of persuasion between the two types of promotion differ greatly. The first are governmental units whose approval is necessary if the institution is to come into existence and receive assistance. The second target consists of those individuals and organizations who are legally entitled to use the new institution but may refrain from doing so because they do not understand it, fear its risks, or are unable to access it.

I encountered both situations when I worked with the Lao government in the mid-1990s to develop a new company law for the country.

Institutional Enactment Promotion

In 1975, the Pathet Lao, an armed communist political movement, forc-
ibly took control of Laos, a small Southeast Asian country that had once
been a French colony. It proceeded to introduce one-party government
and a highly statist economic system, while eliminating the remnants of
French law, including its company legislation. By the 1990s, Laos was
experiencing serious economic difficulties, so it began negotiations with
the World Bank for financial assistance. The bank agreed to help on condition that the Lao government adopt a series of reforms to liberalize
its economy and encourage foreign investment, including the passage of
a new company law. The Lao Ministry of Justice established a working
group to prepare a new company law and asked me to advise it.

The working group consisted of five Lao government lawyers, pri-
marily from the Ministry of Justice. Having taught corporation law
during the eight years that I was a dean and faculty member of Southern
Methodist University Law School, having practiced corporate law for a
few years with a New York City law firm, and having written about corporate governance in Europe and developing countries, I felt that I could
best serve the working group by acting as a sounding board and source of
information on various approaches to corporation law rather than as an
advocate for a particular point of view. Lao lawyers, not an American academic, should be the driving force in shaping a corporation law for Laos.
The working group members readily agreed to my approach, noting that
a few lawyers from large international British and American firms with
offices in Hong Kong had already visited Vientiane, seeking to introduce
a British or American style of corporation law, an approach that the Lao
members of the working group considered overly intrusive. Early in our
labors, the group asserted its independence by deciding that the name to
be given to the new law would be the "Enterprise Law," arguing that the
labels "corporation law" and "company law" were unacceptably "capital-
istic." I saw no reason to argue with their choice.

Within two years, the working group had prepared the text of a new
"Enterprise Law" and sent it to the Lao parliament for enactment. On
my next visit to Laos, a member of the working group met me at the
Vientiane airport and told me that the parliament was refusing to adopt

the draft because its members did not understand the law and did not see its purpose. To deal with the problem, he had scheduled me to give a lecture on the law to the parliament's members and staff at the "Party School," an institution created to train party cadres. The next day, I gave a talk and held a series of meetings on the important role that a corporation law would play in an economy like Laos, which was seeking to encourage local private enterprise and foreign investment. Eventually, parliamentary resistance abated so that the law was ultimately enacted.

The reason for the Lao parliament's change of heart was probably not just the words of a foreign professor but also the "conditionality" of the World Bank's loan to Laos. The bank did not pay the principal amount of its loan to the Lao government in one payment but rather in a series of "tranches" ("slices") spread over time, with each tranche being conditioned on the government's completion of certain specified actions and reforms. At the time the Lao parliament was considering the Enterprise Law, the bank was scheduled to pay a tranche of its loan to the Lao government but was indicating that it might delay payment until the law was passed. In that situation, the leaders of the governing party probably let the members of the parliament know of their strong support for the Enterprise Law, leading the parliamentarians to vote for its passage.

Invariably, politics in any country will influence the enactment of an institution. Institution builders should devise their institutional enactment promotions accordingly. As the working group was in the final stages of completing the Enterprise Law, the Lao economy minister had met with the group to urge completion as soon as possible. When I asked him the reason for the rush, he simply sighed, shrugged his shoulders, and said "conditionality," clearly referring to but not specifically mentioning the conditions that the World Bank imposed upon its loans to Laos.

There are numerous other ways that one may promote the enactment of a new institution. In 1974, when I was serving as the Ford Foundation's Middle East advisor on law and development, the government of Egypt under President Anwar Asad asked the foundation for assistance in instituting the government's new policy of *infitah* or openness, which reversed the policies of his predecessor Gamal Abdel Nasser by seeking to liberalize the Egyptian economy and opening it to foreign investment.

After lengthy discussions, the foundation and the Egyptian government shaped a multifaceted program of support to the Egyptian government to aid in the development of its nascent "openness" policy over the next three years. Specifically, the program contained four distinct elements of assistance that promoted the policy's enactment. They included:

1. A resident team of economic advisers and a lawyer who would work for over three years with the Egyptian government's departments concerned with developing policies and regulations on foreign investment.
2. The visit to Egypt of Harvard University's Professor Edward S. Mason, a renowned expert on economic development, to meet with the Egyptian government's principal policy makers working on issues of economic liberalization and foreign investment for discussions on resolving various problems that the new policies entailed.
3. Visits by Egyptian officials to countries like Ireland, which had enacted laws and policies that successfully attracted foreign investment, to learn how those policies had been developed and implemented.
4. Conferences and training programs to be held in Egypt and the United States for Egyptian officials and professionals in the private sector working on matters relating to foreign investment.

Unlike the preparation of the Lao Enterprise Law which touched only one relatively narrow policy area, Egypt's efforts to open its economy to foreign investment affected many policy areas and therefore required a multifaceted program of support. The program of activities supported by the Ford Foundation over five years helped to advance Egypt's "openness" policy by supporting the development of institutions necessary for its success, including a government ministry responsible for attracting and regulating foreign investment and new laws and regulations governing foreign capital.

Institutional Use Promotion

Even though a country's government may have enthusiastically enacted a new institution, numerous factors may cause its population to avoid using that institution, thereby frustrating the attainment of its policy goals. Anticipating similar problems in implementing the new Enterprise Law in Laos, the working group planned several activities to educate the country's judges, lawyers, and relevant civil servants about the law's provisions. To support these efforts, they asked me to write a simple manual on the law that would be translated in the Lao language and issued with the new law's text when it was enacted. This and other educational efforts successfully diffused the knowledge of the Enterprise Law to important elements of the Lao society and helped to strengthen and broaden its use in the country. As a result, the Lao Enterprise Law remains in force today. The law also led to the creation of yet another new institution several years after its enactment—the Vientiane stock market in the country's capital.

Generally, institution builders need to be aware that, even after an institution has been enacted, the people for whom it was intended may not use it. Three obstacles may prevent that use: (1) people's perception of risk, (2) cultural practices and beliefs, and (3) technical problems. Let's explore each one.

1. Perceptions of Risk

People will be reluctant to use institutions, especially when they are new, if they fear that doing so will subject them to certain dangers. This phenomenon was encountered during the "Green Revolution" in the mid-20th century, which introduced new agricultural techniques in many countries in a successful effort to increase crop yields significantly. At the beginning of these efforts, some small farmers were reluctant to adopt the new techniques because their ability to feed their families depended on their harvests, and they were reluctant to gamble on the success of new untested methods when failure meant that their families would go hungry. In time, as they saw their neighbors have bumper harvests, the reluctance of these farmers faded away as their perception of risk diminished and they increasingly adopted the technologies of the Green Revolution.

More recently, governments creating institutions requiring their populations to undergo mandatory vaccinations against specified diseases encountered similar opposition because of perceptions of risk by people refusing to be vaccinated. They refused vaccinations because they feared the vaccine would ruin their health or kill them. Overcoming opposition to institutions based on perceptions of risk requires institution builders to undertake patient and well-designed programs of public education with no guarantee of success.

2. Cultural Practices and Beliefs

Cultural beliefs and practices are often obstacles to the adoption of new institutions by people that they are designed to serve. The fate of Northern Nigeria's Penal Code, discussed earlier in this book, is a clear example of this phenomenon. In 1999, nearly 40 years after its enactment, 11 heavily Islamic states in the north of the country decided to repeal the code because politicians had convinced them that the code was "unislamic." In other parts of the world, efforts by governments to increase the participation of women in the financial system by encouraging them to open bank accounts were hindered by husbands and bank managers who considered the practice to be against their customs and traditions. The lesson that these and similar cases teach is that institution builders should understand local customs and how to deal with them as they undertake the institution-building process. One way to overcome these obstacles is to recruit a famous person or authority figure to make public statements, assuring people that the new institutions will not injure them or violate their customs and traditions. For example, a political leader or sports personality might be vaccinated publicly to demonstrate that the vaccine is safe and does not violate the country's customs and cultural values.

3. Technical Problems

Modern institutions often rely on, or assume the existence of, modern technology to function. If the underlying technology should fail, the effect may be to destroy public confidence in the institution itself. During the U.S. government's rollout in 2010 of the Affordable Care Act, known commonly as "Obama Care," the website and computerized system for enrolling clients in the program proved unable to handle the large number of potential applicants. Denied access to the system, millions of potential members gave up the effort or deferred it for a later date. This flaw did not kill the new institution, but it certainly gave it a serious wound from which it was fortunately able to recover. Institution builders relying on technology to operate their new institutions to influence human behavior need to be sure that the technology works.

Conclusions: Institution Builder's Promotion Tools

1. Savvy institution builders anticipate the possible reluctance by people to use a contemplated institution and therefore formulate a program to promote it as part of their plans for building their institutions.
2. Institutional promotion efforts should focus particularly on four factors: (1) easing people's fears of the institution, (2) giving people clear understanding of the purpose of the institution and how it works, (3) assuring people that the new institution does not violate their customs and practices, and (4) making sure that the technology to access the new institution is robust and easily usable by the people it is intended to serve.

CHAPTER 11

Task #7: Negotiating Knowledge

Knowledge is the fuel that drives institutions. The knowledge required may be highly complex as the econometrics needed by a central bank to calculate a country's economic trends for the next five years and as relatively simple as knowing how to lay a slab of concrete sidewalk under the guidance of a foreman constantly admonishing workers to "watch and learn, watch and learn." Regardless of the degree of complexity of the knowledge needed by an institution to function, the job of an institution builder is to endow the institution with the means to do three things: (1) to gain the knowledge it needs, (2) to use that knowledge effectively, and (3) to update its knowledge as circumstances require. The pursuit of each of these goals requires institution builders to negotiate.

Gaining the Knowledge

For an institution builder, the task of gaining the needed knowledge for an institution may be as seemingly simple as hiring the right person for a job or as complex as building, equipping, and staffing a five-story biotechnology laboratory. While building a lab is always complex, hiring the right person for the job can be equally complex if that person is a Nobel laureate tenured at Oxford University with multimillion-pound research program. In my first job after law school, I learned something about finding and obtaining knowledge.

We were seven Peace Corps lawyers who went to Nigeria in September 1963. All of us were young, in our mid- to late 20s. Most had just graduated from law school, although a couple had one- or two-years' experience in practice. When we landed in Lagos, then Nigeria's capital, in the early evening after a day's flight from London over the red-brown glare of the Sahara, none of us knew exactly what we would be doing in Nigeria or where we would be doing it. In retrospect, my decision to go to Nigeria reeks of spontaneity, if not recklessness.

In my last year at Harvard Law School, I felt that my own legal education was pushing me inexorably, machine like, in the direction of a law firm in a big city, perhaps New York—a prospect that I simplistically concluded was "just not interesting." In March 1963, less than three months before graduation, the inspiration that I had been looking for arrived. Notices posted around the law school announced the visit of the Peace Corps' General Counsel, William Delano, who was to talk about a new Peace Corps program to send lawyers to Africa.

The Peace Corps, then less than two years old, had been one of the most successful programs launched by President John F. Kennedy's New Frontier. It had captured the imagination of many Americans, particularly recent college graduates, who felt an impulse to serve others and who were inspired by Kennedy's challenge to "ask not what your country can do for you but what you can do for your country." In its early years, Peace Corps volunteers had worked mainly in primary and secondary education, agriculture, public health, and community development in third-world countries. The idea of sending lawyers to Africa was therefore a novel one. Some might even say it was ridiculous. After all, for countries whose biggest problems were poverty, malnutrition, illiteracy, and disease, what did lawyers—American lawyers with little or no practical experience, at that—have to offer?

The prospect of American lawyers working in Africa apparently intrigued many of my law school classmates as much as it did me. When I arrived to hear Delano's talk, the room was already filled so I had to stand at the back. Delano spoke about the state of African development and how the continent's legal systems were emerging just as their political and economic systems were. Africa needed law to assure stability, democracy, and economic growth. The process of legal development would benefit from Peace Corps volunteers who could offer their special skills and energies, working under the supervision of senior Africans. The Peace Corps had therefore established the African Regional Lawyers Project to send about 25 American lawyers to five African countries—Nigeria, Liberia, Ethiopia, Nyasaland (later called Malawi), and Sierra Leone—to work in legal education, judicial training, legislative drafting, and legal administration. He stressed the importance of developing new laws and institutions for the new nations of Africa and that the skills and energies of young American lawyers could help in this process. As I listened, I distinctly remember thinking, "Now *this* is interesting"—as if all the other jobs open to Harvard Law School graduates in 1963 definitely were not.

After that meeting, I applied almost immediately to join the Peace Corps. Just before graduation, the U.S. government informed me that I had been accepted into the African Lawyers Program and would probably go to Nigeria. After spending the summer at a training program at Columbia University for Peace Corps volunteers going to Nigeria and then attending a two-week seminar on African law for the lawyer volunteers at Yale Law School, the seven of us arrived in Lagos with no idea of what we would be doing and where in the vastness of Nigeria we would be doing it. The Peace Corps volunteer who met us at the Lagos airport gave me one clue: "I heard that you and McCarthy are going to the North."

Within a week, Tom McCarthy and I were flying in a Nigeria Airways Fokker Friendship turboprop to Kaduna, the capital of the Northern Region. The trip north took less than two hours, but more than 500 miles of territory seemed to separate Lagos from Kaduna. If Lagos, the commercial and political capital of Nigeria, was crowded, noisy, exuberant, and constantly in motion, Kaduna, when we landed at the airport with its unpaved airstrip, seemed spacious, quiet, and empty. Surrounding the city, the land was flat and vividly green since the rainy season had not yet ended. Here and there on the horizon, gigantic rock formations, small hills really, seemed to spring right out of the earth. These savanna lands stretched several hundred miles north to the Sahara Desert and were the traditional grazing lands of the Fulani tribe's herds of sinewy, long-horned white cattle, a few of which were lingering on the fringes of the airport. While Lagos had been humid so that you always seemed to perspire, Kaduna, we discovered as we walked from the plane to the tin-roofed terminal, was hot but blessedly dry.

Once in Kaduna, McCarthy and I had instructions to call John Burnett, the Northern Region Commissioner of Native Courts in the Ministry of Justice, to receive our assignments. Burnett, a courteous, articulate English barrister, had been working in the ministry since before independence. The Northern Region, like the other areas of Nigeria, had a dual system of courts: One structure tended to follow the English pattern and dealt with important cases covered by English law, as well as serious crimes, and the other structure, referred to as "native courts," handled all other matters. The native courts applied Islamic law and the customary law of the non-Islamic areas in all civil cases. They also tried criminal cases according to the Northern Region Penal Code and Code of Criminal Procedure. The native courts, located throughout the Northern Region in cities and towns, villages, and hamlets, probably handled about 80 percent of the region's court cases. None of its native court judges, who in Islamic areas were known as *alkalis*, had university law degrees, although many had received Islamic legal education or special training of one sort or another. The native courts were the foundation for the administration of justice—indeed for the peaceful public administration and maintenance of order—in the north. Their legitimacy and effectiveness in their role of settling disputes and punishing crime resided in the fact that they were firmly based on the traditions and community values of the Northern people. The judges had the respect and support of the people they served. To preserve that status, the law prohibited lawyers from practicing in the native courts. As commissioner of native courts, Burnett's job was to see that they functioned properly, followed the law, and upgraded the skills of their judges and clerks through inspections and training.

The day after our arrival in Kaduna, we met with Burnett at the Ministry of Justice where he briefed us on the North's legal and judicial system and took us to meet with the Attorney General and Solicitor General, both of whom were British, and the Minister of Justice, a northern Nigerian named Nassir. Afterwards, Burnett explained that he had identified two jobs for Peace Corps lawyers, one with him in the administration of native courts and the other at Ahmadu Bello University in Zaria, a city some 50 miles to the north, where the region's first university law school was being established. As he spoke, I knew immediately that I wanted to work in the ministry. There, I felt, I would be close to the action and have an opportunity to become involved directly in development. Life at the university, on the other hand, seemed too distant, too theoretical, too removed from the realities of Nigeria, and, yes, too academic. How was I ever to contribute to change from the confines of a university? I knew that McCarthy, a big, good-humored Saint Johns' Law School graduate who had specialized in trial work, would also certainly want to work in Kaduna with Burnett. So, how was the choice to be made? Before we had a chance to state our preferences, Burnett told us that our assignments had already been decided. McCarthy was to stay in Kaduna, and I was to go to Zaria. "The dean of the law school," Burnett told me, "thinks you will be happy there." I left the meeting disappointed and a little annoyed. Just how exactly did the dean, whom I had never met, know what would make me happy?

The dean of the law faculty returned from leave a few days after my meeting with Burnett. Alan Milner, a soft-spoken Englishman with a PhD from Leeds University and an LLM from Yale an advanced graduate law degree, had established Ahmadu Bello University's law faculty. Its LLB degree program had just completed its first year with a grand total of six law students. The reason there were so few was that the North had thus far only produced a trickle of secondary school graduates with the qualifications and desire to study law, and the Northern Region government refused to allow more than one-half of the LLB program's student body to come from the south, one more evidence of Nigerian tribal politics. In his quiet way, Milner was a strong academic leader who had a clear vision for the school and was determined to create a law faculty of high academic standards. As the faculty's founding dean, he was also an effective institution builder. During my time in Zaria, he was a constant source of support. He also turned out to have been right. I was indeed happy at the university.

At our first meeting, he described the work he wanted me to do: Teach in the alkali program, run the moot court and legal writing program for second-year students, help organize a new Diploma in Law program to be conducted in cooperation with the University of London for the most educated of the young native court judges and clerks, and, next year, teach the course on Nigerian family law and inheritance for LLB students in their final year. This last assignment surprised me. I knew next to nothing about Nigerian family law and inheritance. Indeed, as a Harvard law graduate with aspirations for corporate practice, I did not know much about American family law and inheritance either. Besides, from my meager understanding of Nigerian law, I knew that family law and inheritance was tribal law. Much of the applicable law was not written down any place. It was based on the unwritten customs of the many different tribes in Northern Nigeria. It apparently was not to be found in any library, and libraries were the only places in which I knew how to do research in law. Just where, I asked Milner, was I supposed to find this Nigerian family law and inheritance so that I could teach it? He smiled and shrugged, "Get thee to the bush."

We agreed that during the current academic year, when my other duties permitted, I would make a series of research trips to various parts of Northern Nigeria to gather information on the customary law of various tribal groups so that I would be ready to teach the family law and inheritance course to LLB students in their final year of the degree program. Here, then, was an institution in need of knowledge to achieve its goal. namely, to teach students a required course in Nigerian family law and inheritance so that they might graduate on time. Milner knew that the only way the school could acquire that knowledge was to go out to the field and find it. Like any skilled institution promoter, he must have seen something in my CV that told him I might be able to solve his institution's knowledge problem. So, he had shrewdly persuaded Burnett to send me to Ahmadu Bello University because *I* would be happy there, certainly a slick bit of negotiation since he was the one who was happy because he had finally found someone to teach a required course in the LLB program.

With the help of the staff at the university's Institute of Administration, I selected five tribal areas in which to conduct my research on customary family law. After developing a questionnaire that would guide my research when I visited the area's courts, after studying whatever anthropological writing that I could find on the chosen areas, and after securing written introductions from the Ministry of Justice to the judges I hoped to interview, I would drive to the area of my research, usually in a Land Rover that I borrowed from the USAID team working at the institute. The drive usually took the better part of a day over dirt roads. Since the areas I was studying were in remote rural location with no hotels or other urban amenities, I would stay in a sparsely furnished mud building that had been designated in colonial times as a "Government Rest House" and continued to bear that name after independence. It was a place where government officials would stay on their infrequent visits to the areas of my research. I was always the only resident in the building.

During my visit, I would spend three to four days interviewing judges, court officers, and scribes and reviewing court records. The courts were usually located in traditional mud buildings with rough wooden furniture. In addition to one or more judges, each court had a scribe who summarized the proceeding in each case by hand in a large ledger. For me, these ledgers in each court that I visited became a gold mine of information on the area's customary family law since they revealed how the courts applied the custom in practice to real cases. I spent long hours copying their contents, knowing that the case summaries would be useful for teaching my course the following year.

After completing my research trips about a year after I began them, I compiled my findings and case summaries into a monograph of 115 pages entitled *A Selective Survey of Nigerian Family Law,* which the USAID team at the institute published in a bound volume for distribution to university students and the courts of the Northern Region. Through this somewhat complicated process, we were able to produce the knowledge needed by the Ahmadu Bello University Faculty of Law to carry out its function of teaching students and diffusing information about the region's legal system. When I returned to the United States in 1965, I left behind at the law faculty in Zaria a detailed syllabus and multiple copies of the *Survey,* hoping that whoever followed me would build on the knowledge that I had accumulated. At the end of 1966, Butterworths, a British publisher, brought out *Nigerian Family Law,* a comprehensive legal text that I coauthored with Alfred Kasunmu, then a lecturer-in-law at the University of Ife in Western Nigeria and later to become one of the country's leading lawyers, thus ending my adventures in Nigerian family law.

Conclusion: Institution Builders' Knowledge Tools

1. As the institution builder, you have the responsibility to secure all the knowledge that your institution needs to perform its function, even if that knowledge is beyond your own expertise.
2. To secure the necessary knowledge, find and commit people who have the needed knowledge to serve the institution.
3. If you can't find experts, find people with the relevant background and abilities and help them to become experts in the knowledge needed.

CHAPTER 12

Finishing Touches

Every new structure requires a "finishing touch"—a final coat of paint, a site clean-up, or a last walk-through to make sure all the building's systems are in working order. Institution builders also need to give their creations a finishing touch to be sure that the institutions they create can function in the way they were designed.

The purpose of this book has been to give you, as an institution builder, a systematic approach to institution building and to suggest tools that you can use to attain your institutional goals. The seven tasks outlined in order in this book are a roadmap that an institution builder may follow from the start, which launches the building process, to the finish, when the institution is endowed with needed resources and is ready to function. Because each step in the process requires the cooperation of other people, the skill of negotiation is the key to securing that cooperation and therefore to establishing the institution. The aim of those negotiations is to create relationships among the parties engaged in building the institution. Virtually all institutions rest on a complex network of human relations. Lengthy detailed contracts may be part of the structure of an institution, but those contracts will not endure if they are not sustained by effective relationships among the parties. An institution builder's final task is to be sure that the relationships underlying the new institution are in place and able to function.

Simply put, a relationship is a sense of connection between two or more people characterized by needed cooperation and a flow of information required to carry out a common task. Relationships do not suddenly and mysteriously come into existence. They are the product of sustained and conscious human interaction. Relationships are not static like clauses in a contract. They are organic and fluid, evolving over time in response to changing circumstances and the actions of the parties. Once you have signed a contract, you will have to work to maintain and strengthen the relationships you have negotiated. Nearly 300 years ago, Francois de Callières, a distinguished French diplomat, gave a similar advice in one of the first practical manuals of modern diplomacy, *On the Manner of Negotiating With Princes*,* in which he stressed the "the necessity of continual negotiation"[1] between states through their permanent representatives as the basis of modern diplomacy. It was a novel idea at the time but one that modern diplomats take for granted today. Modern institution builders should do no less.

As an institution builder, you also need to negotiate strong relationships among your institution's members to build a robust institution and then to manage it. Institutions whose members have strong productive relationships tend to function more effectively than institutions wracked by internal conflict. Like Chief Justice John Marshall leading the U.S. Supreme Court, building negotiating relationships among your institution's members should be a vital part of your role. How should you create the relations necessary for your institution? Here are three simple, but necessary, rules to start with.

1. *Recognize the need for relationships.* You need to accept that relationships are not extraneous niceties but instead are a vital part of building the institution you are seeking. Your actions and communications should be driven by that belief.

2. *Do ask, do tell.* Relationship building between the parties concerned requires transparency and mutual knowledge. Just as the parties need to get to know one another in the negotiation of any long-term transaction, institution builders need to do the same. A policy of don't ask, don't tell is not conducive to relationship building. Indeed, institution builders working together should do just the reverse: Do ask and do tell.

---

* F. de Callières. 1716. *De la manière de négocier avec les souverains. De l'utilité des négociations, du choix des ambassadeurs et des envoyés et des qualitiés nécessaires pour réussir dans ces emplois* (Amsterdam: Pour la Compagnie). The book has been published in many languages since it was written. The most recent English language version is Francois de Callières, *On the Manner of Negotiating With Princes*, trans. A.F. Whyte. 2000, with introduction by Charles Handy (New York, NY: Houghton Mifflin).

3. *Invest time.* Building a relationship takes time. You should therefore be prepared to invest time in negotiating the relationships you are seeking to build your institution, which include attending countless meetings, social events, and one-on-one encounters where you can get to know your colleagues well and they can get to know you.

Notes

Chapter 1

1. North (1990).
2. Ben Ali and Kramer (2016).
3. Machiavelli (1916).
4. World Bank Worldwide Governance Indicators (n.d.).
5. North (1990), p. 118.
6. Salacuse (2013).

Chapter 2

1. Smith (1996).
2. Glennon (2003), pp. 2–28.
3. Smith (1996), pp. 286–287.

Chapter 3

1. Salacuse (2013).
2. See For example, Hampson (1995), pp. 1–51, 345–360.
3. For a history of Goldman Sachs and its decision to go public, see generally Endlich (2000).

Chapter 4

1. See generally, Salacuse (2006).

Chapter 7

1. OECD (2003).
2. Wells and de Royere (2006), p. 2.
3. For a detailed discussion of this case, see generally Salacuse (2022), pp. 333–391.

Chapter 9

1. Quoted in Wilson (2000), p. 197.

Chapter 12

1. *On the Manner of Negotiating With Princes* (2000), p. 6.

References

Ben Ali, M.S. and S.M.S. Kramer. 2016. *The Role of Institutions in Economic Development* 2.

Endlich, L. 2000. *Goldman Sachs: The Culture of Success*. New York, NY: Alfred Knopf.

Glennon, M.J. 2003. "The Case That Made the Court." *Woodrow Wilson Quarterly*, pp. 20–28, Summer.

Hampson, F.O. 1995. *Multilateral Negotiation: Lessons From Arms Control, Trade, and the Environment*, pp. 1–51, 345–360. Baltimore: Johns Hopkins University Press.

Machiavelli, N. 1916. "Chapter VI." *The Prince*, translated by W.K. Marriot. Macmillan.

North, D.C. 1990. *Institutions, Institutional Change, and Economic Performance* 3, p. 118. Cambridge University Press.

OECD. 2003. *Privatizing State-Owned Enterprises: An Overview of an Overview of Policies and Practices in OECD Countries* 3.

On the Manner of Negotiating With Princes. 2000. Ttrans. A.F. Whyte, with introduction by C. Handy, p. 6. New York, NY: Houghton Mifflin.

Salacuse, J.W. 2006. *Leading Leaders: How to Manage Smart, Talented, Rich, and Powerful People*. New York, NY: AMACOM Books.

Salacuse, J.W. 2013. *Negotiating Life: Secrets for Everyday Diplomacy and Deal Making* 2. Palgrave Macmillan.

Salacuse, J.W. 2022. "Anatomy of an Investor-State Arbitration: The Case of *Aguas Argentinas*." *The International Lawyer* 55, pp. 333–391.

Smith, J.E. 1996. *John Marshall: Definer of a Nation*, pp. 286–287. New York, NY: Henry Holt.

Wells, L. and A. de Royere. October 30, 2006. *Aguas Argentinas: Settling a Dispute*, p. 2. Harvard Business School Case no. N9-705-019.

Wilson, J.Q. 2000. *Bureaucracy: What Governments Do and Why They Do It*, p. 197. New York, NY: Basic Books.

World Bank Worldwide Governance Indicators. n.d. https://info.worldbank.org/governance/wgi/.

About the Author

Jeswald W. Salacuse is Dean Emeritus and Distinguished Professor Emeritus of the Fletcher School of Law and Diplomacy at Tufts University. The author of 20 books, his many leadership positions include serving as dean of two university graduate schools, president of three national professional organizations, chair or lead director of 15 different investment companies, president or member of 5 international arbitration tribunals, and an institution builder in over 40 countries. His rich experience animates his book.

Index

Affordable Care Act, 98
Aguas Argentinas S.A. case, 55–56,
    61–69, 75
Authenticity, 50

Bilateral investment treaties (BITs),
    63–64
Bilateral negotiation, 23–27

Capitalization, 72
Civic institutions, 5
Cultural beliefs, 98
Cultural practices, 98

Enterprise Law, 94–95
External negotiation, 22–23

Faculty governance institution, 7–11
Fundraising, 72

Governmental institutions, 5

Human resources, 71–72

"The ICSID Convention," 59
Incremental institution builders,
    17–20
Institutional enactment promotion,
    94–96
Institutional promoters, 40–41
Institution builders, 3
    defined, 13
    in history, 15–17
    incremental, 17–20
    negotiation strategies, 90–91
    preliminary strategies and tactics,
        11–12
    qualities of, 13–15
Institution building
    collective action, 6
    leadership, 37
    negotiation (*see* Negotiation)

principles, 6–7
process of, 5–7
tasks, 33–37
tools, 5–6
Institution-building team, 41–44
    building, tools for, 20
    first meeting, 44–46
Institutions
    aim of, 1–2
    categories, 5
    characteristic of, 2
    country's governmental system
        six factors of, 3–4
    defined, 1
Internal negotiation, 22–23
International Centre for Settlement of
    Investment Disputes (ICSID)
    case, 55–60, 68–69, 73

Leadership, 12, 27, 37, 72–73
Legal negotiation, 35–36, 83–84
    corporate existence, 84–86
    with governments, 86–87, 90–92
    tax exemption case, 87–90

Multilateral negotiation, 6, 23–27

Negotiation, 19
    bilateral, 23–27
    defined, 6
    external, 22–23
    Goldman Sachs' case, 27–29
    institutional enactment promotion,
        94–96
    institutional plan, 34–35
        Aguas Argentinas S.A. case,
            55–56, 61–69, 75
        factors influencing, 55
        International Centre for Settle-
            ment of Investment Disputes
            (ICSID) case, 55–60, 68–69,
            73

tools, 69–70
vision to, 55–56
institutional resources, 35
  categories, 71–72
  and leadership, 72–73
  nature, 71–72
  new sources, search for, 80–81
  sources, 73–77
  tools, 77–79
institutional use promotion, 96–97
  cultural practices and beliefs, 98
  risk perceptions, 97–98
  technical problems, 98–99
nstitutional vision, 34
  authenticity, 50
  role, 47–48
  shaping, 49, 53
  source, 48
  statement, 50
  tale of, 50–53
  tools, 53
institution legalization, 35–36,
    83–84
  corporate existence, 84–86
  with governments, 86–87,
    90–92
  tax exemption case, 87–90
institution promotion, 36, 93–99
interests, 21–22
internal, 22–23
knowledge, 36–37, 101–108
leadership, importance of, 27
multilateral, 6, 23–27
positions in, 21–22
process launch, 33–34, 39–40
  institutional promoters, 40–41
  institution-building team, 41–44
  preliminary agenda, 44
  preparatory measures, 44
  tools, 46
tools, 29–31
Negotiation knowledge, 36–37,
    101–108

Obama Care. *See* Affordable Care Act

Physical resources, 71
Plan negotiation, 34–35
  Aguas Argentinas S.A. case, 55–56,
    61–69, 75
  factors influencing, 55
  International Centre for Settlement
    of Investment Disputes
    (ICSID) case, 55–60,
    68–69, 73
  tools, 69–70
  vision to, 55–56
Precedent, 48
Privatization, 61–66, 68, 69, 80
Process launch negotiation, 33–34,
    39–40
  institutional promoters, 40–41
  institution-building team, 41–44
  preliminary agenda, 44
  preparatory measures, 44
  tools, 46
Public–private partnership (PPP), 66

Renegotiations, 90
Resources
  negotiation, 35
    categories, 71–72
    and leadership, 72–73
    nature, 71–72
    new sources, search for, 80–81
    sources, 73–77
    tools, 77–79

Social institutions
  types, 2

Team building, 14

Vision, 34
  authenticity, 50
  role, 47–48
  shaping, 49, 53
  source, 48
  statement, 50
  tale of, 50–53
  tools, 53

OTHER TITLES IN THE CORPORATE GOVERNANCE COLLECTION

John Pearce, Villanova University, Editor

- *Navigating the Human Side of Boardroom Interactions* by Thomas Sieber
- *Business Sustainability* by Zabihollah Rezaee
- *Corporate Sustainability* by Zabihollah Rezaee
- *A Primer on Corporate Governance* by Jose Luis Rivas
- *A Primer on Corporate Governance* by Andrea Melis and Alessandro Zattoni
- *A Primer on Corporate Governance* by Sibel Yamak and Bengi Ertuna
- *Managerial Forensics* by J. Mark Munoz and Diana Heeb Bivona
- *A Primer on Corporate Governance* by Jean Chen
- *A Primer on Corporate Governance* by Felix Lopez-Iturriaga and Fernando Tejerina-Gaite
- *A Primer on Corporate Governance, Second Edition* by Cornelis A. de Kluyver
- *Blind Spots, Biases, and Other Pathologies in the Boardroom* by Kenneth Merchant and Katharina Pick
- *A Director's Guide to Corporate Financial Reporting* by Kristen Fiolleau, Kris Hoang and Karim Jamal

Concise and Applied Business Books

The Collection listed above is one of 30 business subject collections that Business Expert Press has grown to make BEP a premiere publisher of print and digital books. Our concise and applied books are for...

- Professionals and Practitioners
- Faculty who adopt our books for courses
- Librarians who know that BEP's Digital Libraries are a unique way to offer students ebooks to download, not restricted with any digital rights management
- Executive Training Course Leaders
- Business Seminar Organizers

Business Expert Press books are for anyone who needs to dig deeper on business ideas, goals, and solutions to everyday problems. Whether one print book, one ebook, or buying a digital library of 110 ebooks, we remain the affordable and smart way to be business smart. For more information, please visit www.businessexpertpress.com, or contact sales@businessexpertpress.com.

Printed in the USA
CPSIA information can be obtained
at www.ICGtesting.com
CBHW070326120524
8389CB00018B/225